EGLI-11/89

4

⑤

D1072026

ARCHITECTS OF THE ABYSS

ARCHITECTS OF THE ABYSS

The Indeterminate Fictions of
Poe, Hawthorne, and Melville

DENNIS PAHL

University of Missouri Press
Columbia, 1989

Library of Congress Cataloging-in-Publication Data

Pahl, Dennis.
  Architects of the abyss : the indeterminate fictions of Poe, Hawthorne, and
Melville / Dennis Pahl
    p.   cm.
  Bibliography: p.
  ISBN 0–8262–0707–3 (alk. paper)
    1. American fiction—19th century—History and criticism. 2. Poe, Edgar Allan,
1809–1849—Criticism and interpretation. 3. Hawthorne, Nathaniel, 1804–1864—
Criticism and interpretation. 4. Melville, Herman, 1819–1891—Criticism and
interpretation. I. Title.
PS377.P34   1989   88–39967
813'.3'09—dc19   CIP

FOR MY PARENTS,
DAVID AND DORIS PAHL

CONTENTS

PREFACE

The readings of Poe, Hawthorne, and Melville included in this book constitute, for the most part, an antithetical approach to understanding nineteenth-century American fiction. Instead of trying to assimilate these writers' fictions in the manner usually taken by literary critics—by discovering the truth of the text in its underlying unity or meaning—I am interested in showing how these fictions, in radically ironic ways, go about making the very idea of "truth" problematic.

I begin by challenging Charles Feidelson's influential view of American Renaissance writing as a symbolic language that corresponds to a transcendental truth, that is, a language equivalent to, in Emerson's words, "God's architecture."[1] Indeed, throughout this study I want to insist that the fictional works of Poe, Hawthorne, and Melville, with their ultimately critical stance toward poetic language, consistently undermine any argument for their unity and self-presence. Despite even the ostensible metaphysical aims of these writers—Poe's desire for a literature of "unity" and "totality," Hawthorne's attempt to tell "the truth of the human heart," and Melville's search for the narrative form that would portray "the great Art of Telling the Truth"—their fictional works, I argue, nevertheless prove to be self-subversive.[2]

In each of the readings, I am concerned with the way in which these fictions dramatize the failure of interpretation on the part of a "central consciousness" within the narratives and thus how these fictions become what Paul de Man might have described as "allegories of unreadability."[3] Mirroring while at the same time ironizing the critic's own interpretive ploys to unify the text, and thus establish it as an architectural totality, these fictions will inevitably have precarious implications for *all* readings.

Some will no doubt complain that viewing the fictions of Poe, Hawthorne, and Melville as indeterminate is a way of promoting a kind of nihilism in literary studies or, from another perspective, of reintroducing a formalist aesthetics with regard to American literature. I would argue that

---

1. Ralph Waldo Emerson, *Journals of Ralph Waldo Emerson*, ed. Edward Waldo Emerson and Waldo Emerson Forbes, vol. 2, p. 446. For the connection between Emerson's organic theories of writing and nineteenth-century American notions of architecture, see F. O. Matthiessen, *American Renaissance: Art and Expression in the Age of Emerson and Whitman*, pp. 140–52.

2. The quotations are from, respectively, Edgar Allan Poe, review of Hawthorne's *Twice-Told Tales*, in *The Complete Works of Edgar Allan Poe*, ed. James A. Harrison, vol. 13, p. 153; Nathaniel Hawthorne, preface to *The House of the Seven Gables*, in *The Complete Works of Nathaniel Hawthorne*, vol. 3, p. 13; and Herman Melville, "Hawthorne and His Mosses," in *Moby-Dick*, ed. Harrison Hayford and Hershel Parker, p. 542.

3. See especially the essays in Paul de Man's *Allegories of Reading: Figural Language in Rousseau, Nietzsche, Rilke, and Proust*.

my readings have neither of these implications. First of all, my use of a Nietzschean epistemology (apparent throughout the study) to come to terms with what I consider to be most radical about these fictions does not hold out the conclusion that there is nothing real or knowable or true in the world but rather directs us to answering the questions: What are the interpretive forces that bring truth into being? What is the nature of these forces? How do they represent a will to power on the part of the interpreter-critic-creator? Like Nietzsche's project for deconstructing such metaphysical concepts as truth and error, good and evil, justice and injustice, the fictions of Poe, Hawthorne, and Melville are not truth-giving but rather dramatize the genealogy of truth, with *truth* defined in terms of selfhood, morality, and social justice.

Any argument for a formalist aesthetics that would seek to establish the self-containment or self-referentiality of these fictions must also be dismissed, if for no other reason than that the "truth" of these texts, always being a function of interpretation, necessarily requires the active participation of the critic (despite how his criticism would paradoxically displace the truth at the same time as it figures it forth). Moreover, the way in which these fictions *imply* the interpretive activity, and the way in which interpretation fragments and violates the seeming "purity" of the text, would also rule out any possibility of viewing these fictions in the context of a formalist aesthetics.[4]

Though I am, in essence, posing myself against a traditional New Critical stance toward nineteenth-century American fiction, I must say that I am nonetheless greatly indebted to certain New Critical methods of close reading, as is evident in my concentration on matters of point of view, narrative authority, imagery, and irony. Also extremely helpful to my interpretations were several formalist and thematic studies, including Charles Feidelson's *Symbolism and American Literature*, Edward H. Davidson's *Poe: A Critical Study*, Frederick Crews's *The Sins of the Fathers: Hawthorne's Psychological Themes*, and Lawrance Thompson's *Melville's Quarrel with God*. All these works have provided numerous useful insights into the fictions I analyze.

More properly connected with my own critical perspective are those recent studies in American literature that have been influenced by poststructuralist thought, among them John Irwin's *American Hieroglyphics*, John Carlos Rowe's *Through the Custom House*, Joseph Riddel's "The 'Crypt' of Edgar Poe," Kenneth Dauber's "The Problem of Poe," and Edgar Dryden's *Nathaniel Hawthorne: The Poetics of Enchantment*. These works, as well as the theoretical writings that inform them—that is, the

4. For a fully developed argument against such claims of self-referentiality in poststructuralist analyses of this kind, see Barbara Jones Guetti, "Resisting the Aesthetic."

work of Roland Barthes, Jacques Derrida, Paul de Man, Jacques Lacan, and Michel Foucault—have been instrumental in the development of my ideas.

Several people have made important contributions to the writing of this book. First of all, I want to thank Fred See, who provided many suggestions and criticisms that enabled me to put this book into its present shape. I am grateful for his willingness to listen to my ideas and to share with me his wealth of knowledge about American literature. Henry Sussman and Neil Schmitz graciously read and commented on the manuscript in its various stages of development; their keen insights proved invaluable. I am especially indebted to Kenneth Dauber, whose graduate seminar in nineteenth-century American literature first brought to my attention many of the philosophical complexities in Poe, Hawthorne, and Melville. The following friends, teachers, and colleagues helped me to clarify my thoughts as well as lent moral support: Joseph Fradin, Raymond Federman, Jeannie Walton, Jack Farber, Jeanne Holland, Shari Zimmerman, Alex Indik, and especially Yonat Shimron. Maureen Ries, of Susquehanna University, typed the manuscript, and I would like to express my appreciation to her as well. Most of all, I want to thank my parents, David and Doris Pahl, whose love and support throughout the years have made it altogether possible for me to pursue this project. It is to them that I dedicate this book.

A slightly different version of chapter 2 appeared as "Recovering Byron: Poe's 'The Assignation'" in *Criticism* (Spring 1984); and a version of chapter 3, "Poe/Script: The Death of the Author in *The Narrative of Arthur Gordon Pym*," appeared under the same title in the *New Orleans Review* (Fall 1987). I am grateful to the editors of these journals for kindly granting me permission to reprint.

D.P.
Lewisburg, PA
April 1988

INTRODUCTION

At least as far back as the important study by Charles Feidelson, Jr., *Symbolism and American Literature* (1953), nineteenth-century American fiction has been distinguished for its essentially epistemological themes, that is, for its tendency to dramatize man's longing to "strike through the mask" of inscrutable nature and to see the world in its naked reality, as an unmediated presence. As Feidelson argues, the archetypal figure that seems to have preoccupied the imagination of the writers of this period was that of "Man Seeing, the mind engaged in a crucial act of knowledge."[1] And indeed, when we think of the characters that inhabit the literary landscapes of the three most prominent fiction writers of the American Renaissance—Edgar Allan Poe, Nathaniel Hawthorne, and Herman Melville— we begin to realize how many of these characters are involved in trying to "read" into the dark mysteries of the universe (and often, we should add, for the main purpose of peering narcissistically into the depths of their own selves). It is precisely this romantic dream of *knowing* the truth of nature, and thereby the true nature of oneself, that we see being depicted in Arthur Gordon Pym's exploration into the primitive regions near the South Pole, in Hawthorne's attempt in the Custom House to discern the real meaning of the scarlet letter, and in Ahab and Ishmael's respective quests for the ever elusive white whale. But what is the end result of such epistemological dramas? What truths are finally revealed, not only for the characters in the stories but for the reader as well?

In the following studies of individual texts by Poe, Hawthorne, and Melville, I have tried to show how the specific problems of interpretation that certain fictional characters confront often parallel our own problems of interpreting and how the failure on the part of these characters to arrive at any determinate meaning serves only to mirror our own futile attempts to uncover the supposed "truth" of the literary text. The central focus for each of the writers that I consider is, ultimately, the nature of reading itself. Much in the fashion of Friedrich Nietzsche (and Nietzsche's present-day adherents Jacques Derrida, Paul de Man, and Michel Foucault), these nineteenth-century American writers demonstrate through their work that reading does not help to expose some hidden depth of meaning but rather covers with a new layer of language what is *already* an interpretation, all of

---

1. Charles Feidelson, Jr., *Symbolism and American Literature*, p. 5. For a discussion of the way in which epistemological concerns become important to later American writers such as Henry Adams and Henry James, see John Carlos Rowe, *Henry Adams and Henry James: The Emergence of a Modern Consciousness.* In my epilogue I note that James's epistemology may be seen as an extension of that found in the American writers who flourished in the middle of the nineteenth century.

which implies that there is no bottom, no ground, to the abyss of signification. It is, as my studies attempt to illustrate, within this permanent abyss
that "truth" locates itself, whether that truth be given the name of "selfhood," "morality," or "social justice," as in the works of Poe, Hawthorne,
and Melville respectively.

It may be important to point out that the sort of indeterminacy that
seems to be operating in these fictions is not anything like the
"inconclusiveness" that Feidelson sees as inherent in the symbolic language of American romanticism and, moreover, may even be said to act as
a critique of such a symbolist perspective.[2] Though it is true that Feidelson
goes far in investigating the many paradoxes in the literary language of
these writers, his investigations, lacking the benefit of recent language
theory, must inevitably fall back on the New Critical theories of organicism
and of the formal unity of the text. For Feidelson, the imaginative writings
of Poe, Hawthorne, and Melville (as well as of Ralph Waldo Emerson and
Walt Whitman, with which his study is also concerned) employ a symbolic
language that attempts to discover within contradictory elements an
"absolute unity," thus allowing the creative work to serve as a bridge
between subject and object, between man and nature.[3] Ultimately theo-
logical in tenor, Feidelson's study would see the American romanticists as
having succeeded in capturing a spiritual essence, a totality, within the
ever shifting meaning, or *process*, that is implicit in their writings. Their
"God," he suggests, "is the present reality of [their] work, the process that
unifies all contradictions."[4]

But to assign to these works this kind of metaphysical status—where
finally the work itself becomes a symbol—is perhaps to overstate the influence of Emersonian idealism and of the whole organicist school of thought
on American fiction writers. Hawthorne's "letter" and Melville's "whale"
may appear, for instance, to carry the full weight of symbolism because
they cannot be assimilated to any rational order of meaning; but when we
examine more closely the way in which these alleged "symbols" are
treated within the works, we begin to doubt the potential they have for
ever effecting a happy union between mind and matter (or the natural).
The "rag of scarlet cloth" that Hawthorne discovers in the Custom House
may seem to possess a "deep meaning," or what Feidelson calls an
"inconclusive luxuriance of meaning."[5] But any claim to its corresponding
to a transcendental truth, to a living presence, is at once made ironic by the
fact that, rather than returning us to a state of nature, the letter merely

2. Feidelson, *Symbolism and American Literature*, p. 74.
3. Ibid., p. 69.
4. Ibid., p. 74.
5. Ibid., p. 15.

points to another text that is its real "depth," that is, to the old Surveyor Pue's manuscript of the story of the scarlet letter that Hawthorne finds beneath the *A* and that, after reading, he decides to refashion in the form of his romance. We can thus say, more generally, that whatever meaning the scarlet letter seems to have resides completely *within* the various interpretations that happen to be given to it, whether those interpretations are supplied by Surveyor Pue, by Hawthorne, or by the different members of the Puritan community who wish to impose on Hester Prynne (the letter's wearer) a moral value. Like the letter, the novel itself does not represent some self-possessed truth that needs only to be disclosed by an ideal reader or by, as Hawthorne would say, "the one heart and mind of perfect sympathy."[6] On the contrary, the novel *is* its many readings—or rather misreadings—and these include not only those of the critics but also the one of Hawthorne's known as "The Custom-House," the introductory chapter that could be said to constitute its own commentary on the novel.

Similarly, when considering Melville's figure of the giant and mysterious whale, we come to understand that Moby Dick does not in any way transcend the myriad stories that are told about him but is in fact nothing but those stories, those interpretations—be they historic, scientific, religious, or literary—that altogether remove the figure from the realm of the natural. By the same token, we should recognize that the literary critic's act of reading would serve only to contribute to the mythologizing of Moby Dick, adding another "story" to the one Ishmael has already told. It is such stories, such falsifications as these, that make up the real "essence" of Melville's novel.

If symbolism is, as Feidelson asserts, a "theory of knowledge,"[7] then it is one that—at least in the context of these nineteenth-century fictions—fails in its promise to establish an organic relationship with the world and thus to allow man to become, in Emerson's words, "a transparent eyeball," able to gaze on nature's richness in a completely unmediated way.[8] Any sort of communion with nature would be made impossible by the sheer fact that once man begins to interpret, or use language, he cannot help but distort or disfigure the object of interpretation, corrupting it as he does with a "new" falsifying structure of his own. No matter how "poetic" the language, no matter how much it appears to give itself over to images derived from nature, language will always be belated, secondary (and not a "second nature," as Emerson might argue[9]) to the thing itself; its error

6. Nathaniel Hawthorne, *The Scarlet Letter,* in *The Centenary Edition of the Works of Nathaniel Hawthorne,* ed. William Charvat, Roy Harvey Pearce, and Claude Simpson, 1:3.

7. Feidelson, *Symbolism and American Literature,* p. 50.

8. Ralph Waldo Emerson, *Nature,* in *The Collected Works of Ralph Waldo Emerson,* ed. Robert E. Spiller and Alfred R. Ferguson, 1:10.

9. Ralph Waldo Emerson, "The Poet," in *Collected Works,* 3:13.

will be the *only* "truth" of that thing that is interpreted. As Nietzsche says
in *The Will to Power*: "There are no 'facts-in-themselves,' for a sense must
always be projected into them before there can be 'facts.'"[10]

Such a will to knowledge (or power) on the part of the interpreter can
thus never escape a certain violation of—and violence against—the truth.
So we are not surprised to find Melville's epistemology to be so determined by a metaphorics of violence, as witnessed for instance by Ahab's
desperate attempt to "*strike* through the mask" of Moby Dick or by Ishmael's remarks on trying to comprehend the whale: "True, one portrait
may *hit* the mark nearer than another, but none can *hit* it with any consid-
erable degree of exactness" (emphases mine).[11] Poe's tales may also be said
to characterize truth-seeking in a decidedly violent manner, sometimes
presenting a narrator/reader who recounts events that, very curiously,
culminate in his own tragic death. As the case of Arthur Gordon Pym or
that of the narrator of "MS. Found in a Bottle" clearly demonstrates,
"knowledge" can come in the form of "some never-to-be imparted
secret, whose attainment is destruction."[12] For Hawthorne too, the act of
reading is no less problematic, as it continually fails as a means of achiev-
ing the sort of "true relation" or "intercourse" for which Hawthorne seems
always, in his prefaces, to be nostalgically yearning. The notion of the
"Gentle Reader" who would be capable of grasping sympathetically the
total meaning of a text (without, that is, destroying any part of it) becomes
for Hawthorne no more than an unattainable ideal; as the narrator of *The
Marble Faun* says, to discover how the threads of a text are knitted together,
the reader must necessarily engage in "tearing its web apart. . . . [A]ny
narrative of human action and adventure—whether we call it history or
romance—is certain to be a fragile handiwork, more easily rent than men-
ded."[13]

That interpretation, as these writers define it, will invariably miss the
mark, will distort and deform whatever is being interpreted, suggests to
us that "reading" closely follows the structure of irony, exposing as it does
the permanent gap that exists between word and thing. But the radical
nature of reading here is perhaps not fully comprehended until one recognizes that the reader, who seems to be the primary point of reference for
"making sense," is himself an interpretive problem. What is this self, this
subject that stands before the world, trying to decipher its depths? If we
are to believe Emerson's "Experience," then the self is a unified and sub-

10. Friedrich Nietzsche, *The Will to Power*, trans. Walter Kaufmann and R. J. Hollingdale, p.
301.

11. Herman Melville, *Moby-Dick*, ed. Harrison Hayford and Hershel Parker, pp. 144, 228.

12. Edgar Allan Poe, "MS. Found in a Bottle," in *Collected Works of Edgar Allan Poe*, ed.
Thomas Ollive Mabbott, 2:145.

13. Nathaniel Hawthorne, *The Marble Faun*, in *The Centenary Edition*, 4:455.

stantial entity, a metaphysical (or self-present) source of power, a solid base for one's experience of the natural world. Says Emerson:

The great and crescive self, rooted in absolute nature, supplants all relative existence. . . . The subject is the receiver of Godhead, and at every comparison must feel his being enhanced by that cryptic might. Though not in energy, yet by presence, this magazine or substance cannot be otherwise than felt: nor can any force of intellect attribute to the object the proper deity which sleeps or wakes forever in every subject. . . . Thus inevitably does the universe wear our color, and every object fall successively into the subject itself. The subject exists, the subject enlarges; all things sooner or later fall into place. As I am, so I see; use what language we will, we can never see anything but what we are.[14]

The idea expressed here, of a fixed and determining self, is one that no doubt owes much to the romantic philosophy of Samuel Taylor Coleridge, who writes in his *Notebooks*, "In looking at objects of Nature, I seem rather to be seeking, as it were *asking* for, a symbolic language for something within me that already and forever exists, than observing anything new."[15] The sort of divinity that romantics like Coleridge and Emerson felt existed in nature could perhaps be more successfully sought, and recovered, in one's own self—a self that, through its abundant imaginative resources, could manage to bridge whatever gap lay between itself and the world.

But, it should be understood, such a notion of a founding self is not at all what we find in Poe, Hawthorne, and Melville, whose ironical fictions serve only to radically subvert the tradition of romantic idealism within which Emerson seems to work. For these writers the idea of a "true identity" becomes a far more problematic issue, one having very much to do with *how* the "self" is represented or interpreted. Again it may be useful to invoke Nietzsche, who calls subjectivity into question precisely on these "grounds": " 'Everything is subjective,' you say; but even this is interpretation. The 'subject' is not something given, it is something added and invented and projected behind what there is. —Finally, is it necessary to posit an interpreter behind the interpretation? Even this is invention, hypothesis."[16] With the "subject" ("self," "interpreter") being nothing but an interpretation, a fiction, there is obviously no ground on which we can decide truth—there is no bottom to the interpretive abyss. It is just this predicament that Melville seems to be articulating in a well-known passage in *Pierre*, a novel that turns out to be less about self-discovery than about discovering how the "self" is constructed.

14. Ralph Waldo Emerson, "Experience," in *The Collected Works*, 3:44–46.
15. Quoted from Northrop Frye, "The Drunken Boat: The Revolutionary Element in Romanticism," in *Romanticism Reconsidered*, ed. Northrop Frye, p. 10.
16. Nietzsche, *The Will to Power*, p. 267.

The titular hero of Melville's novel has not yet, according to the narrator, been able to produce a great work of art (a book) because he has not taken the trouble to investigate the wealth of material that lies within himself— "he has not yet procured for himself the enchanter's wand of the soul." However, as the narrator goes on to draw the comparison between Pierre's deeply buried self and a mummy that need only be unwrapped to reveal its substance, the substantiality of selfhood is suddenly put in question:

The old mummy lies buried in cloth on cloth; it takes time to unwrap this Egyptian king. Yet, now, forsooth, because Pierre began to see through the first super-ficiality of the world, he fondly weens he has come to the unlayered substance. But, far as any geologist has yet gone down into the world, it is found to consist of nothing but surface stratified on surface. To its axis, the world being nothing but superinduced superficies. By vast pains we mine into the pyramid; by horrible gropings we come to the central room; with joy we espy the sarcophagus; but we lift the lid—and no body there!—appallingly vacant as vast is the soul of man![17]

Pierre (whose name in French means *stone*) may try to penetrate to the very bedrock of his being, to his true essence, but all he can find are the outer layers of himself, "surface stratified on surface." The "self" here does not signify some meaningful depth but only an illusion of depth, one that is entirely of man's making; indeed the "self" is as empty and as artificial as the pyramidal structure in which it seems to be housed. Like the whole "stony" world that we see depicted in *Pierre* (from the Memnon Stone to the Church of the Apostles to the Mount of Titans), the "inner core" of the novel's hero is inextricably bound to what Melville elsewhere calls "the world of lies,"[18] a world that may be said to have its most explicit delineation in the later novel *The Confidence-Man*, where the authenticity or origi-nality of selfhood becomes all but erased in an endless game of role playing.

The idea that the "interpreting subject" (itself an interpretation) cannot locate itself anywhere but within the realm of fictionality may well indicate that much nineteenth-century American fiction—or at least that repre-sented in this study—finds its informing structure in what is called "romantic irony," wherein it is characteristic for the spectator/reader of a scene suddenly to become part of that scene, in effect, to become the spec-tacle. Such a radical kind of irony would never allow for a reconciliation between subject and object, between inner substance and outer form, as the one would be continually turning into the other, the individual con-cepts of "subject" and "object," of "inside" and "outside," becoming

17. Herman Melville, *Pierre, or The Ambiguities*, in *The Writings of Herman Melville*, ed. Leon Howard and Hershel Parker, 7:284–85.
18. Herman Melville, "Hawthorne and His Mosses," in *Moby-Dick*, p. 542.

themselves undecidable. Here, in what appears to be an endless process of irony, where the subject is constantly engaged in its own subversion, there can be no resolution and, as de Man has pointed out in "The Rhetoric of Temporality," "no synthesis." De Man, who would view the matter of romantic irony from a temporal perspective, has argued that such an irony "reveals the existence of a temporality that is definitely not organic, in that it relates to its source only in terms of distance and difference and allows for no end, for no totality. . . . It can know . . . inauthenticity but can never overcome it. It can only restate and repeat it on an increasingly conscious level, but it remains endlessly caught in the impossibility of making this knowledge applicable to the empirical world."[19]

It is obvious that with this sort of never-ending irony in operation there can be no certainty in the literary text, there can be no point of departure, no source for determining the truth. As we shall see, the fictional works of Poe, Hawthorne, and Melville that I consider here all, in one way or another, dramatize this uncanny structural relationship between subject and object, between inside and outside, between spectator and spectacle; and in so doing they also implicate that spectator par excellence, the critic himself, who locked as he is within the prisonhouse of language cannot help but contribute to the error of interpretation.

The first three chapters of this book concern themselves with the way in which Poe questions the notion of a unified, substantial self. Since these chapters constitute a major part of the entire book, I mean not only to relate the importance Poe has for nineteenth-century American fiction in general but also to set the stage for the later discussions of Hawthorne and Melville, whose respective understandings of morality and social justice become intimately connected to the questionable status of the self as narrative authority or as totalizing central consciousness.

In chapter 1, then, I show how the first-person narrator of "The Fall of the House of Usher," somewhat like the literary critic, tries to gain mastery over the house/text, only to discover that the boundaries between himself and the house of fiction that he enters are impossible to determine. Indeed, the world of Roderick and Madeline Usher that the narrator confronts is found to be made up entirely of texts, representations, references—all of which lead him away from, or disfigure, what the story seems to indicate is his true and original self. But if the narrator's "self" turns out to be something that is problematic (or uncanny), it is perhaps because the narrative we are reading is also that way. Poe's story demonstrates that those oppositional structures that critics have traditionally assumed uphold the "House of Usher," that give it a sense of unity—that is, art/science, irrationality/

---

19. Paul de Man, *Blindness and Insight: Essays in the Rhetoric of Contemporary Criticism*, pp. 220, 222.

rationality, romanticism/Enlightenment—are not in any way stable. Like the deteriorating house in the story, these otherwise meaningful structures, incapable of sustaining themselves, collapse in upon one another; in so doing they can be said to call attention to the very "fall" of language. Thus the sort of "poetic" verbal creation that organicists such as Emerson would have likened to "God's architecture," or the literary artwork that Poe himself (following Coleridge) would want to see as a "totality,"[20] becomes in "The Fall of the House of Usher" nothing less than an *uncanny structure*, that is, one without foundation, without unity, without metaphysical presence.

Chapter 2, a close reading of "The Assignation," also demonstrates Poe's abiding concern with issues of selfhood and self-presence, but this time as they pertain to a historic figure, the poet Lord Byron. Whereas most critics have tended to view the story primarily as a hoax, in which Poe very cleverly disguises details of Byron's life (particularly his romance with the Countess Guiccioli), the story has far more serious epistemological intentions; for in a sense the story becomes a meditation on what it means to recover a "life" in language. Can Byron's true self, Poe seems to be asking, ever be disclosed in language? Or would language—or any other mode of representation—dissolve the being that history has come to recognize as Byron? In trying to "read" the life of a historic personage, the first-person narrator, as it turns out, succeeds not in recovering Byron's essence but in covering over *again*—that is, re-covering—what has already been obscured by the many myths that surround this "stranger," as he is designated in the story. Toward the conclusion of my discussion, I show how Poe's "reading" of Byron is in many respects a reading of himself, or a reading of an earlier version of "The Assignation" titled "The Visionary," a text whose beginning paragraphs (edited out of the later work) help to dramatize the loss of origins and the annihilation of the self in writing.

Poe's questioning of selfhood, especially in terms of his authorship, may be seen indirectly in "The Assignation," but it is in his novel *The Narrative of Arthur Gordon Pym* (discussed in chapter 3) that the questioning of his own authority and authorship becomes explicit. From the point of the novel's preface, where we are introduced to a fictionalized Mr. Poe, to the catastrophic end of the narrative (when the narrator-hero Pym seems to meet a violent death in the "embracing cataract"), the idea of an author, or of some unified identity that stands behind and originates the work, is made problematic. By inscribing himself in his book, Poe does not affirm

---

20. For an interesting discussion of Poe's affinities with New Critical theories of contextualism and also with Emerson's concept of "the poet," see R. E. Foust, "Aesthetician of Simultaneity: E. A. Poe and Modern Literary Theory." My argument in this study is that though Poe's theory of poetics sounds a New Critical chord, his fictional practice reveals a Poe that radically subverts notions of unity and totality in the literary text.

his identity but only alienates himself—"dies"—within his own writing; that is, he loses his "self" within a realm of fictionality. Pym, who becomes a double of Mr. Poe, is also inscribed within a world of writing, of textuality, his whole sea adventure being nothing less than a reflection of Pym's futile efforts to attain mastery over himself and thus to move to a point of self-presence, authority, origination.

In chapter 4 I analyze "Rappaccini's Daughter" to see how Hawthorne portrays moral truth completely as a matter of perspective, though with the additional idea that there can be no "proper" perspective (or interpretation) for the reader to rely on. Framing my analysis of the story within a brief discussion of the way in which moral perspectivism operates in *The Scarlet Letter,* I proceed to "read" the story through the eyes of the character Giovanni Guasconti, who because he occupies a position overlooking Beatrice's garden (the story's central scene) *seems* to possess what Hawthorne calls in his preface "the proper point of view." Indeed, though the narrator tells the story in the third person, he allows most of the action to take place through Giovanni's so-called scientific perspective. Like the reader, Giovanni attempts throughout the story to study Beatrice's complicated "nature" to discover whether she is good or evil, tenderhearted or "poisonous." The story's central question becomes, however, not what Beatrice *is* (morally or otherwise) but what sort of interpretive values are used to "poison" both her and the garden she inhabits. Beatrice Rappaccini becomes so difficult to comprehend because Giovanni, as the story's "central consciousness," sees her from contradictory points of view (empirical and imaginative), neither of which can be said to dominate or be more "proper" than the other.

Chapter 5 focuses on Melville's last novel, *Billy Budd, Sailor (An Inside Narrative);* and here I continue my analysis of issues related to morality, this time emphasizing, as Melville does, the sort of violences that are incorporated in those legitimizing powers or systems that attempt to bring into being a sense of "moral truth" and "social justice." I show that the idea of reading *Billy Budd* as a simple allegory of the conflict between good and evil is made problematic by an unreliable narrator, who is either a sly confidence man or someone simply ignorant of the true events about which he is reporting (indeed Melville leaves ambiguous the narrator's moral character, that is, whether the narrator is consciously or unconsciously subverting the truth of his text). Billy is no more innocence incarnate than Claggart is evil incarnate; rather, both characters are products of morally contradictory "outside" readings, or portraits, in a text that purports to be the narrator's "inside" story. Like Vere's legal forms—which contain the very violences they are supposed to control—the narrator's allegorical system for comprehending the "true story" of the Billy Budd affair demonstrates how a certain will to power is required in constructing any "truth," be it social, moral, or literary.

I
POE AND THE QUESTIONING OF SELFHOOD

Representing mingles with what it represents, to the point where one speaks as one writes, one thinks as if the represented were nothing more than the shadow of the representer. A dangerous promiscuity and a nefarious complicity between the reflection and the reflected which lets itself be seduced narcissistically. In this play of representation, the point of origin becomes ungraspable. There are things like reflecting pools, and images, an infinite reference from one to the other, but no longer a source, a spring. There is no longer a simple origin.

　　—Jacques Derrida, *Of Grammatology*

It is evident that we are hurrying onwards to some exciting knowledge—some never-to-be imparted secret, whose attainment is destruction.

　　—Edgar Allan Poe, "MS. Found in a Bottle"

1 DISFIGURATION IN "THE FALL OF THE HOUSE OF USHER"; OR POE'S MAD LINES

In the opening pages of Poe's Gothic tale "The Fall of the House of Usher," the unnamed narrator, traveling on horseback, approaches the dilapidated Usher mansion, the sheer sight of which afflicts him with the profoundest melancholy (similar perhaps to the melancholy that Poe, according to his "Philosophy of Composition," aims to induce in the readers of his work).[1] So overcome with morbidity is he that he is compelled to dismount his horse and reposition himself before the house, hoping by rearranging the "particulars of the scene" to "annihilate its capacity for sorrowful impression." What happens, however, is that from the "precipitous brink" where he stands, the house's image, now "remodelled" and "inverted" in the "black and lurid tarn" below, suddenly produces in him "a shudder even more thrilling than before."[2] Thus the rearrangement of the narrator's position does nothing in the way of winning mastery over the house; the attempt to "reconstruct" it—put it in right order—results in failure.

Coming to Poe's "The Fall of the House of Usher," we as readers find ourselves in a predicament similar to that of the narrator of that tale. For as the latter stands before that strange abode, looking down at its reflection in the mountain lake, so too must we, gazing through the lens of critical inquiry, attempt to reconstruct the "House." Yet must our fate also be the same as that of the narrator-protagonist, who, hoping to orient himself toward the house, discovers only that his "reading" is subject to further distortion, that the remodeling of the house's image in the lake is nothing more than a *mis*reading? Or is it possible, as some commentators would have us believe, that we can uncover the "truth" of the story, that indeed the critic, from his privileged position outside the text, can finally penetrate to the very heart of the "House of Usher"?

The commentary that suggests the story is about the loss of the self or the regaining of the self tends to argue that the house is the site of the narrator's own madness, a place through which he must pass in order to

---

1. Edgar Allan Poe, "The Philosophy of Composition," in *The Complete Works of Edgar Allan Poe*, ed. James A. Harrison, 14:198: "Regarding, then, Beauty as my province, my next question referred to the *tone* of its highest manifestation—and all experience has shown that this tone is one of *sadness*. Beauty of whatever kind, in its supreme development, invariably excites the sensitive soul to tears. Melancholy is thus the most legitimate of all poetical tones." Though Poe is here outlining his theory of poetry, the statement may apply as well to many of his Gothic prose pieces, where "poetic sentiment" becomes an important motif.

2. Edgar Allan Poe, "The Fall of the House of Usher," in *Collected Works of Edgar Allan Poe*, ed. Thomas Ollive Mabbott, 2:398. All future references to "The Fall of the House of Usher" pertain to this edition.

confront—and later either resign himself to or overcome—his alienated self.[3] Such readings, though admirable in their own systems of analysis, often bypass the system already present in Poe's text and end up projecting their own analyses beyond the text and into their own mystification. Pointing to the significance of the "subject" in Poe's story, they generally ignore how Poe formulates that subject, and thus they fall precisely into a metaphysics of presence that the story, as we shall see, denies. Thus, by taking into account the problem of Poe's representation of the subject, we might better understand what is at issue when we invoke such concepts as "selfhood" and "madness." We might better see how such concepts become articulated at the same time that they are disarticulated.

It is perhaps in the passage already alluded to, the opening lake scene, that we may begin to see how Poe's story problematizes the "self." Here the narrator ostensibly sees in the "tarn" the inverted image of the house; but a closer examination of the particular details of the scene reveals a further complication. For Poe strategically situates the narrator at the edge of a cliff, "the precipitous brink," so that the narrator's gaze can be directed down, straight down—at his own reflection. In other words, the house, described in human terms with its "eye-like windows" (398), merges with the image of the narrator, becomes his double. Later, the "haunted palace" of Roderick's song, which seems to double with the House of Usher, is said to stand in the "monarch Thought's dominion" (406); it is described as a "head," complete with luxuriant blonde hair ("Banners yellow, glorious, golden / On its roof did float and flow" [406]) and with eyes ("two luminous windows" [407]). The logic of this imagery suggests that the House of Usher is supposed to represent a human skull, but one that is "haunted" or falling apart (as the poem and the narrator's experience come to indicate respectively). Are we to assume then, as have numerous other commentators, that the disintegrating house is but a portrait of the narrator's own disintegrating mind, a mind perhaps once firmly rooted in rationalist thought?[4] The psychoanalytic interpretations that support this view are

3. Michael J. Hoffman, "The House of Usher and Negative Romanticism," p. 168, sees Poe's nameless narrator as an example of the "negative romantic" who is "left alone in the stormy night, with everything familiar in the environment having been destroyed and swallowed up by the water. There is no place that he can find comfort, no orientation that he can use to restructure the world of chaos in which he at last finds himself." On the other hand, Maurice Beebe, "The Universe of Roderick Usher," in *Poe: A Collection of Critical Essays*, ed. Robert Regan, p. 133, argues that the ending of the story suggests a "return-to-unity." The narrator's "most triumphant creation is the obliteration of his suffering, diffused self in a return to that oneness which is nothingness."

4. Many of Poe's characters ostensibly make the journey from rationality to irrationality, as does for example the narrator of "MS. Found in a Bottle," who begins his increasingly bizarre voyage with "a mind to which reveries of fancy have been a dead letter and a nullity" (*Collected Works*, 2:135). Pym's journey in *The Narrative of Arthur Gordon Pym* may also be seen as a movement from the realm of rationality to that of irrationality.

legion.[5] But such readings tend to reduce the story to an allegory of schizo-phrenia if they do not account for the problems of representation that the story seems to dramatize.[6] For an understanding of the representational aspects of the "self," we may do well to turn to Jacques Lacan's provocative work in psychoanalysis; it is in Lacan's theory of "the mirror-phase" that we may find a useful analogue to some of the operations already at work in Poe's text.[7]

In his essay entitled "The Mirror-phase as Formative of the Function of the I," first written in 1939 and later revised (1949), Lacan theorizes on the development of subjectivity in childhood. He says that between the first six to eighteen months an infant enters the "mirror-phase," wherein the "hommelette" (Lacan's expression for the infant, because the latter is "a little man and also like a broken egg spreading without hindrance in all directions")[8] first begins to sense his own identity from having seen his image in the mirror.

This jubilant assumption of his mirror-image by the little man, at the *infans* stage, still sunk in his motor incapacity and nurseling dependency, would seem to exhibit in an exemplary situation the symbolic matrix in which the *I* is precipitated in a primordial form, before it is objectified in the dialectic of identification with the other, and before language restores to it, in the universal, its function as a subject.[9]

But Lacan is careful to note that the "Ideal-I" (or "total form") that the child confronts in the mirror "situates the instance of the *ego*, before its social determination, in a fictional direction."[10] For as Jean Roussel says in summarizing Lacan, this mirroring should not be regarded as an identifi-cation in the proper sense, "but *as what first makes identification possible.*"

For the child does not recognize an *imago* as such, but is drawn into the programme

5. See Sam Girgus, "Poe and R.D. Laing: The Transcendental Self," p. 308, for an example that uses existential psychoanalysis to argue the narrator's schizoid condition.

6. Leo Bersani, *Baudelaire and Freud*, p. 5, points out some of the limitations of traditional psychoanalytic criticism: "On the whole psychoanalytically oriented criticism has been reductive in two respects: it interprets literature as a system of sexual symbolism, and, cor-relating with this, it re-places the writer within the infantile sexual organization presumably indicated by his preferred symbols." My own argument is that by relegating elements of the story to psychological categories, such readings do little in the way of addressing problems basic to the literary enterprise—namely the problems of language and representation.

7. For other applications of Lacanian psychoanalysis to Poe's fiction, see Lacan's own "Sem-inar on 'The Purloined Letter,'" trans. Jeffrey Mehlman. Also worth noting is Jacques Der-rida's reading of Lacan's reading of Poe, "The Purveyor of Truth," trans. Willis Domingo et al.

8. Rosalind Coward and John Ellis, *Language and Materialism*, p. 101.

9. Jacques Lacan, "The Mirror-phase as Formative of the Function of the I," trans. Jean Roussel, p. 72.

10. Ibid., pp. 72–73.

of a form of himself projected in space, and in that form discovers himself. Thus primary identification is not a relation between two terms but the very matrix in which the terms for future relations are generated. It is what first establishes identity, as the subject, in a mirage, discovers for itself a unity. Man's first recognition of himself is a radical *misrecognition;* here, clearly, it can be seen that identity *is* difference, that the same *is* an other.[11]

The scene of Poe's narrator before the tarn may be said to dramatize just such a "misrecognition." Though the reader is clearly given the impression that the house duplicates the narrator's face, if not his mind, the narrator nevertheless recognizes only the image of the house. This misrecognition is doubly achieved, since the house, even were the narrator to "recognize" his own reflection, offers a self-image that is both distorted and impenetrable. The house stands upside down in the tarn; in Lacan's terms it might well be "an exteriority in which this form [the mirror image] . . . appears to him [the child-witness] above all in a contrasting size that fixes it and a symmetry that inverts it."[12] The "eye-like windows" are "vacant" (398), or visually incomprehensible, thus precluding the possibility of self-recognition or identification. The *vacancy* of the "eyes," taken in another sense—meaning "abandoned" or "not occupied" as opposed to "expressionless"—becomes significant if one considers the traditionally valued position of the eyes as the body's chief means of access to the soul, that is, as the proverbial windows-to-the-soul. In this case, the center of the narrator's being could be said to be missing, absent, having vacated the premises as it were. Witnessing an empty space where a soul once was, the narrator must necessarily fail to obtain an accurate vision of himself.

It is obvious that in this scene Poe draws considerably on the Narcissus myth, though remodeling it to suit his own purposes. But this is not to say that the assumptions that the scene makes about questions of identity alter in any radical way the basic implications of the ancient myth; for one finds in the Narcissus myth a similar kind of misrecognition, a similar articulation (or rather disarticulation) of the self to that found in Poe's story. In seeing his reflection in the pond, the boy Narcissus falls in love with his mirror image, a thing that has no substance but is (as Ovid points out) "only shadow":

[He] finds the boy, himself, elusive always,
Not knowing what he sees, but burning for it,
The same delusion mocking his eyes and teasing.
Why try to catch an always fleeing image,
Poor credulous youngster? What you seek is nowhere,

11. Jean Roussel, "Introduction to Jacques Lacan," p. 68.
12. Lacan, "The Mirror-phase," p. 73.

And if you turn away, you will take with you
The boy you love. The vision is only shadow,
Only reflection, lacking any substance.[13]

For Ovid's Narcissus, as for Poe's narcissistic narrator, identity *is* difference, the same *is* an other. In a second version of the myth—one that has uncanny resonances in Poe's story—Narcissus, mourning the death of his beloved sister, attempts to console himself by pursuing his sister in the mirror image. In "The House of Usher," Madeline may be seen as that sister if we are willing to view Roderick (her twin brother) as a double of the narrator (the Narcissus figure), in which case the narrator, by a process of substitution, wishes like the brother Narcissus to establish unity with his sister self.[14] Such a unity is impossible, as it can happen only in death, a portrayal of which is given at the end of Poe's story, when Madeline "fell heavily inward upon the person of her brother, and in her violent and now final death-agonies, bore him to the floor a corpse" (416–17). Of course Poe reinterprets the myth and in so doing calculatedly distorts (parodies) it in a number of interesting ways. For instance, the narrator-Narcissus escapes with his life, whereas the Narcissus of Ovid's myth does not; and perhaps in a typical gesture of Poe's perverse irony, the brother is suggested to have tried to murder his sister (Narcissus' beloved) by entombing her before her actual death. But apart from these deviations, it is sufficient at this point to realize the story's striking parallels with the Narcissus myth and to recognize that, as J. Hillis Miller points out, "the doubling of [any] brother and sister or of any man and woman of the same generation is the embrace of two desperate clods, detached bits of the substantial earth beneath, trying to recover a lost unity, trying to make a global whole which would encompass space in a theorem proposed between the two."[15]

This lost unity is the self; and in a sense the whole story may be said to demonstrate a quest for the self, for the origin of one's being as it is given its ultimate expression in the sister self, Madeline, a substitute for the lost mother (source of oneself). The narrator comes before his mirror image, the house, penetrates its depths—those labyrinthine passageways and vaults that represent the unconscious—and on route encounters his alter ego, Roderick, and then his deeper, more secret (because encrypted) self, Madeline, whose mysterious silence and remoteness make her all the more compelling as an object of desire. The dramatization of the need to return to some originary state is already suggested in Marie Bonaparte's

13. Ovid, *The Metamorphoses*, trans. Rolfe Humphries, pp. 70–71.
14. That Roderick is the narrator's double is an idea that has long been acknowledged by Poe scholarship and one that I address in more detail later.
15. J. Hillis Miller, "Steven's Rock and Criticism as Cure," p. 26.

psychobiography of Poe, in which she argues that *both* Madeline and the Usher mansion ("Lady Madeline's double") are mother symbols to "Usher-Poe."[16] And it should not go unnoticed that Poe's narrator, in visiting the Ushers, is suggested to be returning to a more primary stage in his life, that of childhood: "Its [the house's] proprietor, Roderick Usher, had been one of my boon companions in boyhood; but many years had elapsed since our last meeting" (398). Concerning his first glimpse of the house, his mirror image, he remarks, "I have said that the sole effect of my somewhat *childish* experiment—that of looking down within the tarn—had been to deepen the first singular expression" (399, emphasis mine).

But perhaps such readings as that stated above, in relating the psycho-dramatic elements of the story, come dangerously close to totalizing the text—as they tend to go no further than relegating the figures of the story to psychological categories (e.g., mother-symbol). Instead, we might see Poe's story as calling attention to its own textual activity, a procedure that would succeed in noting the differential nature of the story as opposed to the containment of the story under a rigid psychological identity.[17] In this sense, we must recognize, as Poe's story does, the unconscious as having the structure of language, or the dream (since the story makes several allusions to the unreality or dreamlikeness of the narrator's experience[18]) as following those laws of the signifier that would operate against any notion of a self-identical or unified meaning.[19]

The lake scene may stand as paradigmatic for the way "doubling" operates throughout the story, the mirror images continually marking differences, not identities. That the narrator's double, the house, is a distortion, or misrepresentation, of himself has already been demonstrated. But the way in which Roderick doubles with the house and thereby with the narrator is a matter that, though already suggested, requires some eluci-

---

16. Marie Bonaparte, *The Life and Works of Edgar Allan Poe: A Psycho-Analytic Interpretation*, trans. John Rodker, p. 249. See also John T. Irwin, *American Hieroglyphics: The Symbol of the Egyptian Hieroglyphics in the American Renaissance*, where the quest for origins in Poe, especially as pertaining to *The Narrative of Arthur Gordon Pym*, becomes a central concern.

17. The kind of textual analysis I refer to, according to Roland Barthes, *Image-Music-Text*, trans. Stephen Heath, pp. 126–27, "endeavors to 'see' each particular text in its difference—which does not mean in its ineffable individuality, for this difference is 'woven' in familiar codes; it conceives the text as taken up in an *open* network which is the very infinity of language, itself structured without closure; it tries to say no longer *from where* the text comes (historical criticism), nor even *how* it is made (structural analysis), but how it is unmade, how it explodes, disseminates—by what coded paths it *goes off*."

18. In the story there are two direct references to the narrator's dreamlike experience: "Shaking off from my spirit what *must* have been a dream" (400) and "I listened, as if in a dream, to the wild improvisations of his speaking guitar" (404). Moreover, the narrator compares his "utter depression of soul" to "the after-dream of the reveller upon opium" (397).

19. This of course is an allusion to Jacques Lacan's theory in *Écrits: A Selection*, trans. Alan Sheridan. It is not my intention to apply a strict Lacanian analysis but only to call attention to the problems of language already implied in Poe's text.

dation; for it is precisely in the way Poe formulates this doubling—in what terms, by what rhetoric—that we may begin to understand the exact nature of the Usher family and of the affliction it suffers.

The obvious parallel between Roderick Usher and the house is their physical deterioration, worsening with each day; and of course the same could be said for Madeline, whose medical diagnosis indicates "a gradual wasting away of the person" (404). The general "gloom" and "melancholy" (397) that pervades the atmosphere of the house also pervades the spirit of its inhabitants. The specific language Poe employs to describe both Roderick and the house is in no way accidental. Just as in the house there appears to be a "wild *inconsistency* between its still perfect adaptation of parts, and the crumbling condition of the individual stones" (400), in the narrator's friend there appears to be "an incoherence—an *inconsistency*" symptomatic of his "nervous agitation" (402). The "*moulded*" destinies (408) of the House of Usher echo Roderick's "finely *moulded* chin" (401). Like the eye-like windows of the house, Roderick's eyes become "vacant" when finally, his illness taking over, "the *luminousness* of his eye had utterly gone out" (411; we recall here the "two *luminous* windows" of the haunted palace, which doubles with the House of Usher). Toward the end of the story, Roderick's face is marked with a "*stony* rigidity" (415), calling up the stones of the house; the fungi on the dilapidated house hang in a "fine tangled *web-work* from the eaves" (400), suggestive of Roderick's hair with its "*web-like* softness and tenuity" (402) (all emphases mine).

The last verbal link between the two is most revealing in that it signals Roderick and the house's kindred relation to textuality. The word *text*, if we explore its etymology, is a kind of web or something woven, from the Old English *wefan*, to weave. According to the *Oxford English Dictionary*, *text* derives from the Latin *textus*, meaning "style, tissue of a literary work (Quintilian), lit. that which is woven, web, texture."[20] The references to woven material in Poe's story come with a calculated insistence. The house is composed of a "fabric [that at the narrator's first glance] gave little token of instability" (400). Roderick's hair has a "wild gossamer *texture*" (402); and "he could wear only garments of a certain *texture*" (403) (emphases mine). The interior of the house is characterized by "the sombre tapestries of the walls" and the "fretted [interlaced] ceiling" (400, 401).

The textual landscape we observe here can have only serious consequences for the narrator's quest for an originary state. The "house of being" that he has penetrated, being nothing other than a house of fiction, leads him astray instead of allowing him access to himself. The confrontation with textuality, far from offering self-knowledge or "meaning," results only in further misrecognition, that is, in experiencing the radical

20. *The Oxford English Dictionary* (New York: Oxford University Press, 1987), 2:238.

otherness of the mirror image. The "self" as a transcendental signified is deferred. As Roland Barthes points out about the function of textuality:

The Text . . . practices the infinite deferment of the signified, is dilatory; its field is that of the signifier and the signifier must not be conceived of as "the first stage of meaning," its material vestibule, but, in complete opposition to this, as its *deferred action*. . . . [L]ike language, it [the Text] is structured but off-centered, without closure.[21]

Madeline is connected to a certain textuality or writing through her name, a conflation of *made-line* or *mad-line*; that is, a kind of writing that would call attention to its fictive or artificial quality or to its distortion or "madness." Poe's use of conflations in his system of naming (the punning nature of which marks a doubleness on the level of individual words) also becomes significant for Roderick and in doing so redefines his relationship to Madeline. The word *rod* connotes a line, and *rick*, from the Middle English *wrikken*, meaning "to move unsteadily" (the word *wrick* means to twist or being twisted), implies a certain deviation: together, a deviating or *mad-line*. Thus the twins double one another in a way other than by sheer physical resemblance.

The narrator himself is bound up in a kind of textuality that goes beyond his simply being the double of the house-text, for the real source of himself—that which forces this nameless (identity-less) narrator into existence, the "cause" of himself, the motivation for his journey and therefore his narrative—is a letter. It is Roderick's letter that summons him, that indeed may be said to inaugurate the whole episode at the Usher house. The narrator's "beginning" is a letter, a text, and a distorted one at that. As he reports, "The MS. gave evidence of nervous agitation" (398), by which we may infer that the letter had been written in an unsteady hand, leaving behind a somewhat illegible scrawl—mad lines.

In a sense, the narrator's whole journey, both the physical journey and the verbal one, is a series of mad lines, tracks or passageways that twist and turn (as can be expected in the labyrinthine depths of the Usher house), leading to nowhere in particular—or at least to no final goal. Everything the narrator encounters in his progress through the "many dark and intricate passages" (400) represents a deferral of meaning. The gloomy chambers, vaults, "somber" walls, and "ebon" floors (400) lend to the interior an air of impenetrable mystery. The little illumination there is comes from "Feeble gleams of encrimsoned light" (401)—a light that would disfigure any object coming under its glow. The valet who conducts the narrator to Roderick's studio is "of stealthy step" (400), and the family physician who passes on the staircase wears an expression of "low cunning and perplexity" (401). Both parties suggest a deviousness that is difficult to

21. Barthes, *Image-Music-Text*, pp. 158–59.

comprehend, so briefly do they appear and so sketchy is their characterization. In Roderick's private chamber the windows, those passages to the soul that are inaccessible from the outside, are likewise inaccessible from within, so vast a distance are they from the black oaken floor. Moreover, being "long, narrow, and pointed" (401), they are constituted as pointers, or signs, whose references are indefinite—they lead to no determinate meaning or signified. (For signs by definition designate what is absent, what may exist but what at the present is not here.) Thus, once having penetrated, so to speak, the mystery of the house (having entered the house's confines), and now standing on the inside, apparently privy to the secrets of the soul, the narrator is still excluded, an outsider to the "truth" of the house and of himself.

Moving into the center of the Usher house, into its depths, its "meaning," the narrator discovers only detours to the "truth." A central room is Usher's library, which houses a collection of occult books, a genuine list (as scholars have noted) of pseudoscientific, mystical, and quasi-theological texts.[22] Entering this room, the narrator encounters a world of textuality. The centrality, or significance, of this room is at once put in question by the sheer fact of its becoming what Jacques Derrida might call a "scene of writing," a place where one finds only references to other writing and other texts (thus calling attention to the decentering, or deferral, of meaning).[23] Madeline, who also figures as "central" in the story, is strangely absent, making at first only a ghostly appearance, as she "passed slowly through a remote portion of the apartment, and, without having noticed [the narrator's] presence, disappeared" (404). For the most part she is concealed, in a temporary tomb that lies "immediately beneath that portion of the building in which was [the narrator's] own sleeping apartment" (410). If she does indeed represent the narrator's innermost, subconscious self—his "truth," the center of his being—it is one that is well hidden; and if this "self" should ever be resurrected, as it is toward the end of the story, it will be one that remains inaccessible behind its "enshrouded figure." The portrait of Madeline after she rises from the tomb is one of a figure disfigured by the "blood upon her white robes" and by her "emaciated frame" (416).

The deferral of meaning is also dramatized in the various texts or representations scattered throughout the narrative, each one repeating the

22. This sentence is quoted almost verbatim from Joseph Riddel, "The 'Crypt' of Edgar Poe," p. 128. My study, having much in common with Riddel's, departs from his in the way it takes similar issues—concerning origins, duplication, deferral—and develops them with an emphasis on the critic's own relationship with the text.

23. Derrida, "The Purveyor of Truth," suggests that the beginning of "The Purloined Letter," since it "begins" in a library, among texts, references, is a false beginning. As a "scene of writing," Usher's library likewise has no origin, no central point, as texts always refer us elsewhere.

other but with a difference. "The Haunted Palace" and the "Mad Trist," reflecting to a certain extent the events in the house, are fictions-inside-of-fiction, albeit distortions of each other if only because they are formulated differently. "The Haunted Palace" is a song/poem, whereas the "Mad Trist" is something of a medieval romance (or a parody of one). One of Usher's paintings, a "phantasmagoric" conception (405) less abstract than some of his others—and therefore renderable in words—duplicates the house's interior, as well as the "unnatural light" that toward the end of the story enshrouds the mansion (412). Indeed, repeating the house's labyrinthine structure, the painting depicts "the interior of an immensely long and rectangular vault or tunnel"; and because this vault or tunnel is situated "at an exceeding depth below the surface of the earth" (405–6), the painting may be said to symbolize Madeline's tomb as well. The different fictive structures that continually point to or shadow "The House of Usher" (yet another fictive structure)—be they poems, stories, or paintings—form an abyss of mirroring fictions,[24] each one a disfiguration of the other, thus marking what Joseph Riddel calls "a radical secondariness, a discontinuity between image and imaged."[25]

Given the status of texts in Poe's story—their deviating, disfiguring nature—it is perhaps only fitting that such deviations be emblematized in that mad line, that "zigzag" fissure that runs through the house, "from the roof of the building . . . to the base" (417), tracing a path that ends up somewhere in the "sullen waters of the tarn" (400). But if this mad line is to represent the status of textual lines, it must also be seen to represent the status of family lines, for as the story indicates, the House of Usher stands not only for the physical structure but also for the family itself (it is, says the narrator, "an appellation which seemed to include, in the minds of the peasantry who used it, both the family and the family mansion" [399]). Indeed, it is strongly suggested that Roderick's adverse mental condition, a deviation of sorts,[26] stems from a hereditary disease, as he explains to the narrator that it "could be traced to a . . . palpable origin—to the severe and long-continued illness—indeed to the evidently approaching dissolution—of a tenderly beloved sister—his sole companion for long years—his last and only relative on earth" (403–4). That the race of Ushers, of which

24. See Neil Hertz, "Freud and the Sandman," in *Textual Strategies: Perspectives in Post-Structuralist Criticism,* ed. Josue V. Harari, p. 311: "There is no term in English for what the French critics call a *mise en abîme*—a casting into the abyss—but the effect itself is familiar enough: an illusion of infinite regress can be created by a writer or painter by incorporating within his own work a work that duplicates in miniature the larger structure, setting up an apparently unending metonymic series." The mirroring fictions in Poe's text, I am suggesting, form precisely this *mise en abîme.*

25. Riddel, "The 'Crypt' of Edgar Poe," p. 128.

26. I am suggesting that the family "illness" becomes part of the story's rhetorical makeup; it is part of the rhetoric of "disarrangement," as will be discussed.

Roderick seems fated to be the last surviving member, is an incestuous one seems apparent from this last quotation; and one is given additional evidence for this in the fact that "the stem of the Usher race, all time-honored as it was, had put forth, at no period, any enduring branch; in other words, that the entire family lay in the direct line of descent, and had always, with very trifling and very temporary variation, so lain" (399). Indeed, in this family there is a "deficiency . . . of collateral issue" and an "undeviating transmission, from sire to son, of the patrimony with the [Usher] name" (399). Such a rhetoric of directness and straight lines, seeming to contradict the zigzag pattern of the fissure (the mad, deviating line) that runs through the house, must, however, be seen in the light of the paradoxical implication of incest: for it is precisely in the direct, undeviating line of descent that the deviation of incest (or the deviating family line) is constituted.

Another way of formulating this paradox is to say that the familiar suddenly takes on the aspect of the strange; that which is most intimate, as would be relations of incest, is also most bizarre. It is just this sort of paradox that Freud invokes in his 1919 essay entitled "The Uncanny," which because of its comprehensive etymological analysis of the German word *heimlich* (meaning "belonging to the house") seems to have a particular relevance to Poe's story. In the beginning of the essay, Freud offers this definition of the uncanny: "that class of the frightening which leads back to what is known of old and long familiar."[27] An uncanny event need not be terrifying, but as Freud would suggest, when it is, the terrifying feeling is invariably provoked by one's sense of encountering something that is at once strange *and* familiar.[28] The whole notion of the misrecognition-in-the-mirror-image that is thematized in "The House of Usher" may be said to come under the heading of the uncanny. But Poe's story states the terms of the uncanny even more flatly than this: when the narrator is conducted by the valet through the "intricate passages" of the house—which he had been acquainted with since "infancy" (400)—he senses the familiar surroundings as strange. He says, "while I hesitated not to acknowledge how familiar was all this—I still wondered to find how unfamiliar were the fancies which ordinary images were stirring up" (400–401). And in a statement regarding his familiarity with Roderick (who may indeed function as that repressed side of him suddenly emerging as strange), the narrator points out the contradictory nature of their uncanny relationship: "Although, as boys, we had been even intimate associates, yet I really knew little of my friend" (398).

27. Sigmund Freud, "The Uncanny," in *The Standard Edition of the Complete Psychological Works of Sigmund Freud*, ed. James Strachey, 17:220.
28. See Maria M. Tatar, "The Houses of Fiction: Toward a Definition of the Uncanny," p. 169.

No doubt there is a certain element of uncanniness at work in "The House of Usher," and the above quotations would seem to indicate as much; but perhaps the uncanniness of the story is not to be found so much in its "content" as in its structure—a structure that Freud alludes to in his analysis of the word *heimlich*. Here Freud, following the history of the word's usages, discovers that it possesses a double meaning, with one meaning contradicting the other (thus resulting in the word itself taking on an uncanny aspect). Summarizing Freud's analysis, Maria Tatar points out in her essay "Toward a Definition of the Uncanny":

> On the one hand, it [the word *heimlich*] designates that which is familiar and congenial; on the other that which is concealed or kept from sight, and hence sinister. The genesis of this double meaning becomes evident if one reflects on the nature of a house or home. A house contains the familiar and congenial, but at the same time it screens what is familiar and congenial from view, making a mystery of it. Thus it comes as no surprise that the German word for a secret (*Greheimnis*) derives from the word for home (*Heim*) and originally designated that which belongs to the house. What takes place within the four walls of a house remains a mystery to those shut out from it. A secret, for the Germans in any case, literally ex-cludes others from knowledge.
>
> The word *heimlich* is so charged with ambiguity that, in one of its shades of meaning, it coincides with its antonym *unheimlich*. "What is *heimlich* comes to be *unheimlich*," as Freud puts it. But if the two words can figure as synonymous for each other, then the prefix *un* does not, as is usually the case, negate the meaning of the adjective, but functions rather as a "token of repression."[29]

The rhetorical as well as the spatial structures implicit in the notion of *heimlich* have a special resonance in Poe's house of fiction; and it is the marked uncanniness of these structures that serves to put in question those binary oppositions that are usually associated with the story.

Locating such oppositions as rationality/irrationality, science/art, and Enlightenment/romanticism indeed becomes a convenient strategy for making sense of the story, for finding in it a fixed meaning. Michael J. Hoffman, for instance, equating the house with Reason ("Thought's dominion"), gathers from "The Haunted Palace" poem, embedded in the story, that the house's fall is "a metaphor of the decline of the Enlightenment." For Hoffman, then, the house (and the story in general) becomes the site of a confrontation between two distinct historic categories, the Enlightenment and romanticism.[30] Another, more recent article tries to demonstrate that Poe's story is a "parable of defective vision and imaginative timidity," in which the narrator is a "defeated rationalist who has vio-

---

29. Ibid., p. 169.
30. Hoffman, "The House of Usher and Negative Romanticism," p. 165.

lated the kingdom of aesthetics."[31] Such readings are not surprising in light of the traditional assumptions revolving around the sharp division between classicism and romanticism—the former camp being primarily associated with reason and restraint, the latter with the full, if not excessive, exploitation of imaginative resources.[32] In "The Fall of the House of Usher" there is little problem in locating rhetoric that would coincide with either of the two ostensibly competing literary-historic camps.

We need only observe the opening paragraph to discover a set of statements that fit easily into a standard romantic mold. Here the narrator, posing in the conventional form of the melancholy romantic (a stock figure in Gothic fiction), speaks of an "insufferable gloom" that so pervades his spirit it cannot be converted by the mind into "poetic . . . sentiment." The "sickening of the heart" and the "dreariness of thought" he experiences become so profound as to prevent their translation "into aught of the sublime" (397). Of course it is just these untamable emotions that the melancholy romantic fervidly seeks out in his quest for the sublime, that airy, unspeakable realm that is most "poetic" because it is beyond the reaches of poetry. As far as the rhetoric of reason is concerned, we see it displayed most obviously in (as already mentioned) "The Haunted Palace" poem.

In the greenest of our valleys,
    By the good angels tenanted,
Once a fair and stately palace—
    Radiant palace—reared its head.
In the monarch Thought's dominion—
    It stood there!

                    (406)

Hoffman argues that these lines represent a time previous to the decline of reason, shown later in the poem:

These lines present us with a time and place in which Thought reigned supreme. It is a time in which, as in the Enlightenment construct, there is a perfect orientation perceivable by Reason (Thought) between the things of the natural world ("The greenest of our valley") and those of the spiritual realm ("By good angels tenanted"). King Thought reigns in a "radiant palace."[33]

But perhaps the moment in the story when reason (or science) and irra-

---

31. See Frederick S. Frank, "Poe's House of the Seven Gothics: The Fall of the Narrator in 'The Fall of the House of Usher,' " p. 333.

32. For an extensive overview of the traditional distinctions made between romanticism and classicism, see Irving Babbit, *Rousseau and Romanticism*.

33. Hoffman, "The House of Usher and Negative Romanticism," p. 161.

tionality (or art) most forcibly confront each other is the moment just preceding the house's destruction, when the storm approaches the vicinity of the house and when the narrator, to calm Roderick's nerves, reads the story of the "Mad Trist." Indeed, we may say that it is the way these two opposing forces are set up as "causes" for the house's final destruction that constitutes their confrontation. Does the house fall because of natural events or unnatural events? The storm that engulfs the house, with its terrific whirlwind that nearly blows the narrator and Usher off their feet (412), might be taken as a natural reason for the house's demise. But an ambiguity is created in the narrator's suggestion that the storm, though it could have been a "merely electrical phenomenon not uncommon," may also have had its origin in "the rank miasma of the tarn" (413), a place associated with the unnatural (the tarn is said to produce the peculiar atmosphere surrounding the house, "an atmosphere which had no affinity with the air of heaven" [399]). A perhaps more plausible scientific reason for the house's fall is given, even though Poe takes care to "hide" it, burying the evidence, as it were, in an unobtrusive description of the vault where Madeline is entombed:

It had been used, apparently, in remote feudal times, for the worst purposes of a donjon-keep, and, in later days, as a place of deposit of powder, or some other highly combustible substance, as a portion of its floor, and the whole interior of a long archway through which we reached it, were carefully sheathed in copper. (410)

The suggestion here is that the house is brought down by the force of an electrical storm that ignites the combustible substance on the floor and sends a powerful electric current through the copper conductor, thus spreading the explosive forces in a kind of chain reaction through the house. (Though offering this explanation, Poe, it should be added, characteristically undermines it by suggesting the total absence of lightning during the storm, as the narrator carefully observes [412]. Besides putting in question the possibility of an explosion, the absence of "any flashing forth of lightning" also points to the *unnaturalness* of the storm, made visible only by the "unnatural light.")

That the house falls right after the reading of the "Mad Trist" summons a final irrational explanation—the power of imaginative writing. It is clear that the sounds denoted in the interpolated tale ("the breaking of the hermit's door, and the death-cry of the dragon, and the clangor of the shield") are supposed to correspond to the "distinct, hollow, metallic, and clangorous" (415) reverberations made by Madeline's rending of her coffin, a correspondence that, in fact, does not escape Usher's notice. Because of the seeming confusion of events here, one is led to suspect that just as

Madeline's resurrection from her tomb seems to signal the house's utter demise, so too does the reading of the "Mad Trist." Indeed, this may be Poe's way of dramatizing the strength of his own fiction or possibly the power of artistic expression in general. But of course there are other readings, ones that would render quite different implications. For example, G. R. Thompson sees the "Mad Trist" as pure parody—a tale that is made "purposely ludicrous" and whose ironic effect is that "it destroys the Gothic illusion." "As in 'Metzengerstein' and 'Ligeia,'" says Thompson, "Poe intrudes an ironic distance clearly and suddenly between the narrator and the reader, here calling attention to the real psychological situation of the two protagonists engaged in their own mad tryst."[34] In this sense, the tale serves to demonstrate not the positivity of fiction but rather the essential negativity of fiction, that kind of breaking of illusion that is characteristic of romantic irony.

The cause for the house's fall is not easily settled; and one wonders if the binary oppositions just set down—science/art, rationality/irrationality—should be insisted on or if they should instead be subsumed under a broader set of terms that would encompass a greater range of thematic and rhetorical elements. For what becomes more and more apparent as one investigates the particular rhetoric that runs throughout "The House of Usher" are the many references to *arrangements* and *disarrangements*, and how these rhetorical structures at certain moments in the text become enfolded in one another in a most uncanny way. The narrator, for instance, tries to establish a "different *arrangement* of the particulars of the scene" (398); the conditions for what Roderick calls "the sentience of all vegetable things" are "fulfilled in the method of the collocation of these stones—in the order of their *arrangement*, . . . above all, in the long undisturbed endurance of this *arrangement*" (408); at Usher's request, the narrator aids him "in the *arrangements* for the temporary entombment" (409) (emphases mine). *Arrangement* is likewise implied in the rhetoric of science and rationality (already referred to), in Roderick's "finely moulded chin," and in the house's "perfect adaptation of parts" (400). Conversely, *disarrangement* is implied in the mental derangement of the Usher family, in Roderick's and Madeline's deteriorating physical health, and in the house's "crumbling condition" (400).

What the narrator calls the "inconsistency" of the house's condition and of his friend Roderick's manner can likewise be applied to the status of art. For art possesses the strange inconsistency of simultaneously giving form to the world and, because it merely re-presents, taking that form away— *de*forming the world. Indeed, *art* would seem to collapse the "competing structures" of the story, now redefined in terms of arrangement and disar-

---

34. G. R. Thompson, *Poe's Fiction: Romantic Irony in the Gothic Tales*, 95.

rangement. In the text, arrangement suddenly turns into disarrangement—rather *is* disarrangement—in the scene we started with, the opening lake scene. Here the narrator, trying to arrange the scene like a painting—referring as he does to the "particulars of the scene" as "the details of the picture" (398)—succeeds only in disarranging it, in creating a more distorted scene. Such a moment may well serve to dramatize the uncanny dynamics of art.

Another key moment in the text comes after Roderick's singing of the verses of "The Haunted Palace." Here the narrator explains Roderick's obsessive concern with "the sentience of all vegetable things," an opinion that in the course of discussion becomes more exaggerated:

But, in his disordered fancy, the idea had assumed a more daring character, and trespassed, under certain conditions, upon the kingdom of inorganization. I lack words to express the full extent, or the earnest *abandon* of his persuasion. The belief, however, was connected (as I have previously hinted) with the gray stones of the home of his forefathers. The conditions of the sentience had been here, he imagined, fulfilled in the method of the collocation of these stones— in the order of their arrangement, as well as in that of the many *fungi* which overspread them, and of the decayed trees which stood around—above all, in the long undisturbed endurance of this arrangement, and in its reduplication in the still waters of the tarn. (408)

There are several ironies at work in this passage. To begin with, the passage points out that the mere *arrangement* of the particulars of the scene (of the house) is what makes the conditions of sentience possible. What is arranged, however, is a number of things that represent waste or decay— fungi, decayed trees, stagnant water—in other words, the general breakdown in the order of things. Therefore, the "foundation" of this structural arrangement is nothing less than *disarrangement*, a point that is perhaps best dramatized by the arrangement's "reduplication [or distortion] in the still waters of the tarn." That Roderick maintains the existence of life (sentience) in the "kingdom of inorganization" is ironic for more reasons than what is paradoxically asserted here. For Poe's ingenious use of the word *inorganization* is calculated not only to mean inanimate objects (relating to the word *inorganic*) but also to summon the idea of "lack of organization." Thus inscribed in the classificatory system ("kingdom") is the uprooting of that system—in the very word that names the classification! Another unusual usage in this passage is *collocation*, a word ordinarily used to designate, according to *Webster's New Collegiate Dictionary,* "a noticeable arrangement or conjoining of linguistic elements (as words)." The arrangement of stones is thus associated here with the syntax of sentences, the careful arrangement of words, another suggestion perhaps that language, so arranged (as in a poem or story), has a certain lifelike power or sentience. But if the latter *is* suggested, so too is the opposite: accompanying the power of language to put life into an inanimate world is a marked impotence, a failure of language to approximate life. For language, in this sense, precisely arranged, contains as well the disarrangement/decay represented by the fungi overspreading the stones. It becomes the place where "science" merges with "art," "rationality" with "irrationality"; indeed it becomes the very essence of the house, always in a state of arrangement and disarrangement, construction and de-construction.

The undecidability marked by the uncanniness of language (which thus results in the collapsing of binary oppositions) is evident also on the level of spatial structures, most particularly the structure of inside/outside. In the abyssal structures of the house, where enclosures are enclosed within one another, one can no longer distinguish the container from the contained. Roderick's painting is a case in point, as it presents "the interior of an immensely long and rectangular vault or tunnel, with low walls, smooth, white, and without interruption or device" (405). The picture, located in a room in the house (an enclosure within an enclosure) portrays another enclosure that seems to double, or mirror, the space that the picture is located in—the labyrinthine structure of the house's interior. The dizzying effect of this *mise en abîme* is further accentuated by the fact that the picture itself is an enclosure, contained as it is within a frame. And yet what is the picture but one inside of another, since as we've already discovered, the entire house is seen by the narrator as a "picture." But lest we think the house marks the final frame, the ultimate container, Poe's narrator is there to inform us that this is not necessarily so, that the house's frame is a false one. Witnessing the house's "crumbling condition," he says in regard to the general structure of the edifice: "there was much that reminded me of the specious totality of old wood-work which has rotted for long years in some neglected vault, with no disturbance from the breath of the external air" (400). Indeed, the house itself is suggested to be a thing contained, not simply a container, locked away inside a "neglected vault" (perhaps another picture).

In a sense the whole house is a crypt among other crypts, and it is therefore not surprising that the bipolar relation between inside and outside is put in question. But perhaps the questioning of this relation—the kind of uncanniness of the relation as displayed in Poe's story—is already contained in the very notion of a crypt. In a long, meditative essay on crypts, entitled "Fors," Derrida notes:

The crypt is . . . not a natural place, but the striking history of an artifice, an *archi-tecture*, an artifact: of a place *comprehended* with another but rigorously separate from it, isolated from general space by partitions, an enclosure, an enclave. So as to purloin the *thing* from the rest. Constructing a system of partitions, with their inner and outer surfaces, the cryptic enclave produces a cleft in space, in the assembled system of various places, in the architectonics of the open square within space, itself delimited by a generalized closure, in the *forum*. Within this forum, a place where the free circulation and exchange of objects and speeches occur, the crypt constructs another, more inward, forum like a closed rostrum or speaker's box, a *safe*: sealed, and thus internal to itself, a secret interior within the public square, but, by the same token, outside it, external to the interior. Whatever one might write upon them, the crypt's parietal surfaces do not simply separate an inner forum from an outer forum. The inner forum is (a) safe, an outcast outside inside the inside.[35]

If the House of Usher is the crypt we assert it is, then following from the parallels already implied between the story ("The House of Usher") and the physical structure represented, can we not also say that the narrative too is a kind of crypt, one that dissolves the inside/outside opposition? The texts of "The Haunted Palace" and the "Mad Trist" also resemble crypts, embedded as they are in the middle of the narrative; but to suggest that these texts are *inside* the narrative implies a hierarchical relationship, with "The House of Usher" standing on the *outside*, a ground for which the other texts are merely figures. But can we really distinguish between those texts incorporated within the story and the story "proper"? Or do not the texts of "The Haunted Palace" and the "Mad Trist" help to constitute the very narrative of the story "proper"? Given that the various texts and representations stand in analogous relationship to each other, are mirrors of each other, it is difficult to identify the original story (or representation) from which all the rest stem, especially when the "original" itself turns out to be but another mirror. The dizzying implications of such an endeavor are neatly dramatized toward the end of the narrative when a number of stories (texts) converge on one another to form their own kind of "mad tryst." Here the priority of texts is put in question, and as a result we are forced to reconsider a problem that has already been posed: the problem of what finally makes the house fall.

Of the many "stories" that collect at the end of the narrative—the storm, Madeline's resurrection, the "Mad Trist"—not one can be singled out as the actual "cause" for the house's fall, since they all seem to blur together and create a dissonance "like the voice of a thousand waters" (417). Among all the noises—the tempest described in Sir Launcelot Canning's "Mad Trist"; the "actual" tempest that surrounds and threatens to destroy the house; Madeline's breaking out of her crypt, accompanied by the "screaming or grating sound" of her prison door (414); the breaking down of the hermit's door by the "Mad Trist"'s hero, Ethelred; the "unnatural shriek" of the

35. Jacques Derrida, "Fors," trans. Barbara Johnson, pp. 67–68.

dragon in the "Mad Trist"; and the "terrible ringing sound" of Ethelred's shield falling to the floor (414, 415)—the narrator cannot distinguish one sound from another, indeed one story from another, as they all merge in a "mad tryst" of fictions, none of them enjoying a more privileged status than the other. Added to these noises is the dissonant sound—"a long tumultuous shouting sound"—that comes when the house is finally destroyed, its "mighty walls rushing asunder" (417). The inside story (the "Mad Trist") becomes the outside story, and the outside one the inside.[36] The collapse of the inside/outside opposition is in a sense equivalent to the collapse of the house: the structure of the story, like the structure of the house, is always already in a state of collapse. For what is really at stake here, and what the end of the story may serve to dramatize (with its sounds "like the voice of a thousand waters"), is nothing less than the "fall" of language, the way language marks its own failure to apprehend truth (as it calls attention to its own secondariness), canceling out that "presence" of the world that it paradoxically figures forth.

We are left, then, with the question of the narrator's escape from the falling house to a point of safety *outside* the house, away from the "madness" and destruction that the House of Usher (in both its meanings) seems to evoke. But the idea that he does escape, get outside, is immediately put in question by the italicized words at the end of the story—the *"House of Usher"*—which thus announce the story itself as well as the narrator's enclosure within it, that is, within a world of textuality. The story's end does not signal a return to normalcy, to order and wholeness, or a "triumph of reason," as has been contended.[37] Nor does it signal the kind of closure suggested by Georges Poulet's belief: "When sinking into its own pool, the House of Usher disappears into itself. It reabsorbs its space and its duration. It completes, from causes to effects, the closed cycle of its existence and of the existence of its hero [Roderick Usher]."[38] For if the house is finally erased, it nevertheless leaves behind a residue: the narrator himself, who still must witness his own distorted features in the "sullen waters of the tarn." In the wake of the house's destruction, his mirror image remains. That this mirror image is as distorted as ever is suggested by the dissonance that the narrator experiences in the final lines, a dissonance that is described in terms directly relatable to the tarn (reflecting pool): "the voice of a thousand *waters*" (emphasis mine). That the nar-

36. Claudine Herrmann and Nicholas Kostis, "'The Fall of the House of Usher' or The Art of Duplication," p. 41, argue that the end of the story demonstrates the collapse of metonymy and metaphor, which becomes equivalent to the collapse of "the literal and figurative meaning, the container and the contained." Their conclusion—that the sinking of the house in the tarn signals the destruction of duplication—I disagree with.

37. Ibid., p. 42.

38. Georges Poulet, *The Metamorphosis of the Circle*, trans. Carley Dawson and Elliot Coleman, p. 202.

rator's escape is a false one, that he is doomed to dwell forever within the "House of Usher"'s fictive terrain, is suggested by the path he takes away from the house. Disfigured by the "blood-red" moon's "wild light" that shines through the "once barely-discernible fissure" (417), the path is a zigzag line, a mad line, that the narrator follows "out." Not having access to the outside, he remains confined in a world of disfiguration, of fiction: he can never win mastery over the House of Usher because the very language that allows him to construct it also prevents his penetrating its "truth."

Given the seeming circularity of the story, with its title incorporated in the last words, one might be led to view the story as self-contained, or as self-identical, and perhaps to accept Poulet's general estimation of Poe's fiction: "Surrounded . . . by a circumference, reduced to the exact space it occupies, . . . the tale exists only in itself."[39] This of course is to assert the story's own self-mastery, when in fact "The House of Usher," as we have discovered, is a disfigurement of *other* fictions inscribed within it, contaminating its context and subverting self-identity. We have already mentioned how the story possibly disfigures (parodies) the Gothic romance, as well as how it inscribes the Narcissus myth (also disfigured according to Poe's re-reading). But a story not yet mentioned, which finds its way into "The House of Usher" in a striking fashion, is one written by the German romanticist E.T.A. Hoffmann. "The Entail" concerns a hermit named Roderick, of "morose temperament and averse to human society," who lives on a ruined estate that will eventually, during the course of the story, collapse on him. The "sentient" stones in Poe's story may well be compared to "The Entail"'s lifelike stones from which come "unearthly cries and lamentations." Hoffmann's scene in which the servant unexpectedly comes up from the basement, walking in his sleep, while a lightning storm wreaks its fury on the estate, also has resonances in Poe's story when Madeline rises from her basement crypt during the "tempestuous" night. Finally, like the House of Usher, "The Entail"'s family line, which Roderick desperately wants to extend, is said to suffer an incurable affliction:

Poor short-sighted old Roderick! What a malignant destiny did you conjure up to destroy with the breath of poison, in the first moments of its growth, that race which you intended to plant with firm roots to last till eternity![40]

Poe's re-reading of Hoffmann's tale, inscribed within "The House of Usher," demonstrates the way Poe's story transgresses its own frame, breaks through its own textual boundaries, to become other than what it is—the story's family line extending, as it were, to other fictions *outside*,

39. Ibid., p. 201.
40. E.T.A. Hoffmann, *Weird Tales*, trans. J. T. Bealby, pp. 217, 320, 321.

ones different from itself. Indeed this dramatizes well what Derrida means when he says that "in the extent to which there is already a *text*, a network of textual referrals to *other* texts . . . the presumed interiority of meaning is already worked upon by its own exteriority. It is always already carried outside itself. It already differs (from itself) before any act of expression [meaning]."[41] The intertextual nature of Poe's fiction in general, it might be added, can be seen in the way he embeds his *own* tales within each other. And in this regard it should not go unnoticed that "The House of Usher" gets reinscribed in a humorous-satiric story that Poe published in 1845. "The System of Doctor Tarr and Professor Fether" concerns itself with a madhouse, one of a more literal kind than the Usher house but one that is similarly "dilapidated" and that also inspires the narrator with "absolute dread."[42] (Like "The House of Usher," the story begins with the narrator's approach on horseback amid the gloomy atmosphere that pervades the area near the isolated house. Though the story moves in a much different direction from "The House of Usher," the basic structure—with its reversal of the inside/outside opposition—is very similar.)

In the same way that other stories get inscribed in "The House of Usher" or that "The House of Usher" gets inscribed in other stories—thus subverting the story's context, its centrality—so too does a certain shifting of contexts take place within the *same* story. We have already witnessed how the story's name becomes incorporated in the last line of the narrative. But there is another word that changes its context, a word altogether central to the text and without which the story would lose its "identity." Of course we are speaking of the word *usher,* which names the house, the family, and the story itself. Practically hidden (repressed) within the story (like one of the story's many crypts), it appears in lower case only once, and unobtrusively—in connection with the valet, who after conducting the narrator through the house, "now threw open a door and *ushered* [the narrator] into the presence of his master" (401, emphasis mine). Slipped into the text at this point, the "key" word suddenly takes on a marginal status, reduced in significance even by the fact of its lower-case letter *u.* In the present context it is no longer a proper noun but is rather an active verb. Yet though it seems here to be stripped of its importance, one should perhaps see the word in context with its subject, the valet (whose marginality as a character is equivalent only to *usher's* as a word), to understand the full ironic implications of the word's status. For both words are bound up with the idea of metaphor, whose Greek antecedent is *metaphora,* meaning "to transfer, to bear, carry." The word *usher,* in this sense, is easily substituted for metaphor. Since the valet's activity is to conduct, or *transfer,* the narrator

41. Jacques Derrida, *Positions,* trans. Alan Bass, p. 33.
42. Edgar Allan Poe, "The System of Doctor Tarr and Professor Fether," in *Collected Works,* 3:1003.

from one part of the house to the other, he functions as a kind of metaphor. Thus the irony here is that the most marginal character in the story, the valet, turns out to be "central": he points to, or emblematizes, the chief occupation not only of the other characters (whose textual/metaphorical implications we have already discussed) but also of the story itself. Indeed, the valet becomes the metaphor par excellence, the metaphor *of* metaphor, the real *usher* of the tale—thus reversing the hierarchy that places the "main" characters of the story in a privileged position.

The decenteredness of Poe's text, as has been examined throughout this discussion, must have grave consequences for the reader, who is put in a position similar to that of the narrator, able neither to get *outside* (and thus attain mastery) nor to locate himself on the inside. Any reading of the story is doomed to be a disfigurement of the "truth," since we too are locked inside the radical secondariness that language represents. Our reading thus can only mark the ushering in of a new fiction, a new system of mad lines traced over the old, thus extending (and bending) the genealogical line of fiction once again, as "The House of Usher" has already done.

2 RECOVERING BYRON
The Search for Origins in "The Assignation"

Few would deny the presence of Lord Byron in Poe's "The Assignation," even though Byron's name is not once mentioned during the course of the narrative. Indeed, his presence is palpable in many oblique references to his life, poetry, and letters—most of which have been well documented by source-hunting critics.[1] The plot, for instance (as these readers attest), draws its inspiration from Byron's famous romance with the Countess Guiccioli; the story's setting may be seen as an allusion to the fourth canto of *Childe Harold*, whose initial lines read: "I stood in Venice on the Bridge of Sighs / A palace and a prison on each hand"; and the hero is apparently an English poet.[2] Still, with all these traces of Byron's presence, the narrator insists on a certain silence, referring to the mysterious lover of the story simply as the "stranger." Even one of the story's more prominent source-hunters—Richard Benton—admits: "There is no specific clue in the text of 'The Assignation' itself that helps establish the hero's identity. His identity is furnished mainly by connotation."[3] The question remains, why should Poe's story evade making a *direct* reference to Byron? Why does it finally try to cover him up?

Benton's article on "The Assignation" contends that the story is a hoax, a sort of joke Poe played on his readers who were "ordinarily shocked by the Byronic message."[4] The story may well be a hoax (a cover-up), but it is one that has far more serious intentions than the most general understanding of hoaxing would allow; for in portraying Byron "under cover," "The Assignation" reveals itself as a kind of meditation on what it means to recover a "life" in language. In a sense Poe casts himself in the role of biographer, not so much to illuminate Byron's true self as to fathom biogra-

---

1. See especially Roy P. Basler, "Byronism in Poe's 'To One in Paradise,'" and Richard P. Benton, "Is Poe's 'The Assignation' a Hoax?" For additional commentary on the story's background, see Benjamin Franklin Fisher IV, "To 'The Assignation' from 'The Visionary' (Part Two): The Revisions and Related Matters."
2. That the hero also exhibits extraordinary skill as a swimmer indicates a further parallel with Byron, who is noted for having once swum the Hellespont.
3. Benton, "Poe's 'The Assignation,'" p. 197.
4. Ibid., p. 193. Other critics who view the story as a hoax include G. R. Thompson, *Poe's Fiction: Romantic Irony in the Gothic Tales*, p. 127, and Edward H. Davidson, *Poe: A Critical Study*, pp. 138–39. Seeing the story as one in which "Poe turned fooling into art," Davidson goes so far as to link this sort of art with a distinctly American character: "There was in America a very lively encouragement to and actual practice of the lampoon, the hoax, the elaborate jest because of one very salient feature of the American character—the fondness for verbalisms and verbal humor, the skill for developing elaborate verbal tricks and grotesqueries as a means of reducing men to a common democratic denominator or of deflating frauds and phonies."

phy in general, that is, the writing or representation of a life. Here the question of Byron's "presence" in the text becomes a matter not simply of his being nominated in Poe's fictional work but of his being as such. Wherein lies the truth of Byron? Can his essential self ever be fully disclosed in language? Or would language necessarily dissolve the being, the self-presence, that history has come to recognize as Byron?

Problematizing the idea of a fully present self, Poe's text raises questions about language that have been explicitly addressed by present-day theorists such as Jacques Derrida. Derrida's notion that linguistic signs refer themselves only to other linguistic signs, that texts refer only to other texts, results in a proposition that "all language will substitute itself for that living presence of the proper, which, as language, already supplanted things in themselves. Language *adds itself* to presence and supplants it, defers it within the indestructible desire to rejoin it."[5] Such a double gesture, in which presence is unthinkable without language and yet is prevented from securing itself within language, is what marks out the problematic that Poe's text dramatizes. For Poe, as well as for the critics of Poe's text, "Byron" stands as a point of presence, a fixed origin, that vanishes the moment language, or representation, submits itself to its primary activity of interpreting (which it does from the start). Interpretation, as Nietzsche pointed out before Derrida, does not lead to a founding origin or a truth but to that which is itself an interpretation.[6] Poe recognizes this, as Byron becomes precisely that dissemination of writings and mythologies that have been conveniently collected under a proper name.

In a way Poe's "reading" of Byron—the text of "The Assignation"—functions no differently than do other interpretations, including those of critics. In an essay that points out how slight the distinction is between literature and criticism, Eugenio Donato states: "Interpretation [which is Donato's umbrella term for both types of discourse] . . . is nothing but sedimenting one layer of language upon another to produce an illusory depth which gives us the temporary spectacle of things beyond words."[7]

5. Jacques Derrida, *Of Grammatology*, trans. Gayatri Spivak, p. 280.

6. See J. Hillis Miller's explication of Nietzsche in "The Disarticulation of the Self in Nietzsche." Miller notes: "The various entities of the inner world making up a given person's 'character'—feelings, thoughts, volitions, the 'self'—is not a present document waiting to be read. It is created by the act of interpretation which reads it. Interpretation posits signs and reads them, in a single act, once more of autogeneration, autosuspension, and, ultimately, of autodestruction, since any act of interpretation always contains the material of its own undoing. The phenomena of the inner world of character are not facts to be named. They are themselves entities which only exist as hypotheses, that is, as performative suppositions, signs which are interpretive fictions" (p. 256).

7. Eugenio Donato, "The Two Languages of Criticism," in *The Structuralist Controversy,* ed. Richard Macksey and Eugenio Donato, p. 96. Reading would thus invalidate the idea that Byron could stand as an ultimate referent ("beyond words") that would dominate the text. Derrida, *Of Grammatology,* p. 158, argues: "Yet if reading must not be content with doubling

Interpreting Byron, Poe's language effaces the very origin it desires to obtain, an origin that subscribers to the hoax theory have not been inclined to see as problematic. What Poe's text ultimately does is dramatize how interpretation prevents the reclaiming of origins. But as in all interpretations, the origin or truth that interpretation seeks to secure becomes problematic not only with regard to the object of interpretation but also with regard to the interpreter himself.[8] And thus "The Assignation" proves to be as much a quest for Poe's presence as it is for Byron's.

The opening of "The Assignation" makes no secret of the narrator's intention to recover the stranger's life in all its essence—to see the stranger not as he presently is ("in the cold valley and shadow") but as he lived and "*shouldst be*—squandering away a life of magnificent meditation in that city of dim visions, thine own Venice."[9] Yet the narrator takes measures to prevent a full disclosure of the stranger's identity, at moments mocking the reader's exclusion from an unobstructed view of the mysterious man. For instance, after perhaps the most dramatic scene of the story—in which the stranger plunges into the canal to save the Marchesa's child from drowning—the stranger removes "his cloak, heavy with drenching water" and reveals himself to a crowd of "wonder-stricken spectators" as the distinguished person he is: the "young man, with the sound of whose name the greater part of Europe was then ringing" (154). It is part of the narrator's teasing irony that whereas the spectators of the scene are allowed access to the stranger's identity, the reader (who is another kind of spectator of the scene) must remain in the dark.

But it is not enough that the narrator covers up the stranger's identity by omitting significant details, that is, his name; the narrator also represents the stranger, for the most part, as someone who covers *himself* up. Indeed the stranger is portrayed as something of a recluse, occupying a lavishly decorated apartment to which few have gained admission: "With one exception," he tells the narrator, "you are the only human being, besides myself and my *valet*, who has been admitted within the mysteries of these

---

the text, it cannot legitimately transgress the text toward something other than it, toward a referent (a reality that is metaphysical, historical, psychobiological, etc.) or toward a signified outside the text whose content could take place, could have taken place outside language. . . . *There is nothing outside of the text.*"

8. Donato, "Two Languages," p. 96, quotes Michel Foucault's *Nietzsche*, Cahiers de Royaumont, Philosophie, no. 6 (Paris, 1967), p. 189: "'Interpretation will henceforth always be an interpretation by the "who." One does not interpret that which is in a signified but in the last analysis the one "who" has laid down the interpretation. The principle of interpretation is nothing but the interpreter himself.' What begins by being the questioning of a subject inevitably turns out to be an indictment of him who questions in the first place."

9. Edgar Allan Poe, "The Assignation," in *Collected Works of Edgar Allan Poe*, ed. Thomas Ollive Mabbott, 2:151. All future references to "The Assignation" pertain to this edition.

imperial precincts" (159). Too, during much of the scene at the Bridge of Sighs (the site of the child's near-drowning), the stranger obscures himself by standing within the shadows of the prison's architecture, in a "dark, gloomy niche" opposite the Marchesa's chamber window. When he finally emerges from the shadows, he is "a figure muffled in a cloak" (153, 154). And last, it is strongly suggested that the stranger conceals any information that might establish his English identity—that he is, in the words of the narrator, "not only by birth, but in education, an *Englishman*" (164).[10]

What, then, does all this covering up—both on the narrator's and on the stranger's part—mean? Surely there is more at stake than playing a joke on Poe's unsuspecting readers. We need only glance at the relationship between the stranger and the Marchesa, and at the way that relationship is dramatized in the scene at the Bridge of Sighs, to realize that the problem of "covering up" has far-reaching implications—implications that we might designate as epistemological and that cannot help but revolve around the question of representation.

It is obvious that the stranger and the Marchesa are related by their love for one another and also by the deep suffering they experience because of their separation (the Marchesa's marriage to the old, domineering Mentoni is suggested to be the main obstacle to the affair). But the young lovers are related in another way as well. For on examining the particular rhetoric used to describe them, one discovers that the stranger and the Marchesa— like Roderick Usher and his sister Madeline in "The Fall of the House of Usher"—are *mirror images* of each other. Both are seen as "statue-like" (153): the stranger possesses features that are "classically regular" and comparable to the "marble ones of the Emperor Commodus" (156), whereas the Marchesa presents a "classical head" (152) and a "marble countenance" (154). They are both likened to deities: the stranger has "the mouth and chin of a deity" (156), and the Marchesa's other name, Aphrodite, links her to the Greek goddess of beauty. Their eyes are also described similarly, having qualities that render them both "wild" and "liquid" (155, 156).

Thus when the Marchesa gazes on the stranger from the opposite end of the Bridge of Sighs, she witnesses none other than her own strange self. Her longing to unite with the stranger is in a way similar to the sort of psychodrama we see in "The Fall of the House of Usher," where self and other (or image of the self) attempt to achieve a unified identity but can do

10. The stranger's "English identity," as I shall discuss later, is itself made problematic by the narrator's admission to having received a report "involving so many improbabilities" (164). Though we are made to think, at first, that the narrator is somewhat blind to the events and circumstances that surround him, the story here indicates that *the difficulty of knowing*— rather than simply the narrator's particular obtuseness (an obtuseness that some critics attribute to his rational, and hence uninsightful, mind)—is the problem. See note 20 for a further elaboration on the rational/irrational dichotomy that some critics affirm.

so only in death.[11] Here Marie Bonaparte's study of the mother obsession in Poe is much to the point, since such a longing to become *one* with oneself or, in other words, to see oneself no longer repeated in an image, is equivalent to wanting to secure the "mother."[12] In short, to get beyond the doubling that the mirror image achieves is to return to some originary state, which "mother" signifies. As Lacanian psychoanalysis argues, such a return proves impossible, as it would imply the establishment of an undifferentiated self-identity, that is, an identity that can forgo defining itself in terms of its essential otherness—its *difference*.[13] That Poe problematizes the possibility of this return to origins may well be suggested in the difficulty the Marchesa has in locating/seeing/recovering the stranger (her strange self, her double) as he stands hidden in the shadows of the prison's architecture. But it is perhaps in the incident of the child's near-drowning, and subsequent recovery, that the drama of the self's quest for origins—and of all the problems that such a quest implies—is given its most concrete expression.

In this incident, the child slips from the arms of its mother, the Marchesa, and falls into the "deep and dim canal." The narrator reports:

The quiet waters had closed placidly over their victim; and, although my own gondola was the only one in sight, many a stout swimmer, already in the stream, was seeking in vain upon the surface, the treasure, which was to be found, alas! only within the abyss. (152)

As the Marchesa stands only a few steps above the mirror surface of the "quiet waters" into which her child has fallen, the child symbolically becomes that part of herself—possibly her primary self—that is lost or kept strange. The drowning scene becomes another example of how the self loses itself, gets *covered up*, in the mirror image. And even though the treasured self can be "found," such a possibility of recovery is made problematic insofar as the *place* of that recovery—the abyss—indicates a no-place, a depth that is bottomless. This problematic recovery of the self is further dramatized when the child, after being saved by the stranger, is *not* returned to its mother but is instead taken away, presumably at the command of Mentoni:

11. The psychodrama played out in "The Fall of the House of Usher" culminates in the final scene, where Madeline "fell heavily upon the person of her brother, and in her violent and now final death-agonies, bore him to the floor a corpse." Since Roderick and Madeline are mirror images of each other, their final embrace dramatizes an attempt to recover a lost unity.

12. Marie Bonaparte, *The Life and Works of Edgar Allan Poe: A Psycho-Analytic Interpretation*, trans. John Rodker, pp. 261–72, seems to reduce the story to an Oedipal fantasy, though not without suggesting possible avenues of inquiry that I attempt to explore here.

13. See Jacques Lacan, "The Mirror-phase as Formative of the Function of the I," trans. Jean Roussel, pp. 71–77.

But the Marchesa! She will now receive her child—she will press it to her heart—she will cling to its little form, and smother it with her caresses. Alas! *another's* arms have taken it from the stranger—*another's* arms have taken it away, and borne it afar off, unnoticed, into the palace! (154)

Always being mediated (either in the mirror image or, as in the latter case, by intermediaries), the "true self," it seems, can never be recovered; and since the chief metaphor for recovery in "The Assignation" turns out to be *seeing*,[14] it is not surprising that vision is often represented as being distorted or deflected in some way. The Marchesa, for instance, is not look- ing down at the mirror surface of the water where her child (the image of her self) is drowning, as one would naturally expect (surely the narrator finds her behavior "strange"); rather she keeps "her large lustrous eyes . . . riveted in a widely different direction!" (153)—at the stranger who is on the other side of the bridge. The narrator attempts to excuse, or to under- stand, her strange behavior, saying:

Who does not remember that, at such a time as this, the eye, like a shattered mirror, multiplies the images of its sorrow, and sees in innumerable far off places, the wo [*sic*] which is close at hand. (153)

Whatever the rationale for her gazing in a "different direction," her action serves to dramatize a deflection of vision, as if to suggest that the self cannot be *seen*, or known, directly. As already mentioned, the stranger (also an image of the self) is a shadowy figure, difficult to discern; but even aside from his being covered up in ways already described, we discover that the very viewing of him is itself distorted. Indeed, since the large lustrous eyes out of which the Marchesa gazes are "liquid," we are given to understand that everything she sees, she sees without the benefit of direct perception: liquid would mediate in such a way as to distort, bend, refract the line of vision. All objects of her vision become re-presentations. In this sense the narrator may be correct, for different reasons than he discerns, in comparing the Marchesa's eyes to a "shattered mirror."

That the self cannot elude its own representation, its own absence in the mirror image—and hence its own *coveredness*—is plainly demonstrated in the character relationships as they are defined in the first segment of the narrative (the scene at the Bridge of Sighs). It remains for the second half of the narrative—which emphasizes the stranger's point of view—to make

14. The narrator's attempt to *see* the stranger—in the sense of recovering him—becomes nowhere more apparent than when he describes his desire to *remember* the stranger's counte- nance, an issue that will be addressed in more detail later. The story's many shifts in perspec- tive—for example, from the narrator to the Marchesa to the stranger (during the scene at the Bridge of Sighs)—suggest that "The Assignation" is in some way a drama of vision.

explicit the question of representation, especially as it relates to art and originality; for here the idea of locating one's true and original self in some kind of representational art is held up as a possibility that can be nothing less than problematic.

As the self can only be "known" through representation, one is compelled to understand the meaning of the "assignation," or union, of the two lovers in death. Can the self be recovered in spite of its representational aspects (as the separated lovers symbolically yearn to become a unified, substantial self)? One might easily suspect Poe of entertaining the familiar romantic notion that the source of oneself (one's essence, the truth) can be revealed through representation (art). This becomes especially plausible when one considers that the type of death the lovers meet is one that, paradoxically, sustains their life as would art—eternally. To the stranger, death means a fulfillment of his dreams (it is "that land of real dreams" [166]), where he can enjoy everlasting harmony with his beloved. That death becomes associated with art (or that they are implied by one another) is indicated in the lines from George Chapman's *Bussy d'Ambois* that the narrator recites, just before the stranger drinks his poison.

> He is up
> There like a Roman statue! He will stand
> Till Death hath made him marble!
>
> (165)

Death will turn the stranger into a marble statue that will live forever, that will no doubt survive the centuries in the same way the altar of Laughter (which he previously mentioned to the narrator) survived all the other temples and shrines of Sparta (159). But the question remains, can art finally recover, make *present*, the self? Can it offer a truth?

At the end of the story, the stranger unites with beauty itself (Aphrodite), yet despite the idealistic implications, beauty turns out to be no guarantee of truth. Throughout "The Assignation" the very idea of originality (which implies truth) as it pertains to art is made ironic. An obvious example of this occurs in the scene in which the stranger, at his apartment, is promoting the excellence of his fabulous art collection. On hearing the narrator's laudatory comparison of the stranger's painting of the Madonna della Pieta to the Venus of Medici ("she is undoubtedly in painting what the Venus is in sculpture" [160]), the stranger immediately takes issue:

"Ha!" said he, thoughtfully, "the Venus? . . . Part of the left arm . . . , and all the right, are restorations; and in the coquetry of that right arm lies, I think, the quintessence of all affectation. Give *me* the Canova! The Apollo, too, is a copy—there can be no doubt of it—blind fool that I am, who cannot behold the boasted inspiration of the Apollo! I cannot help—pity me!—I cannot help preferring the Antinous. Was it not Socrates who said that the statuary found his statue in the block of marble? Then Michael Angelo was by no means original in his couplet—

'Non ha l'ottima artista alcun concretto
Che un marmo solo in se non circonscriva.'

[The best artist has no concept
which the marble itself does not contain.]" (160–61)[15]

From his discussion it is apparent that the stranger's evaluative understanding of art turns on the question of originality. The uniqueness of his Madonna must be seen in contrast to the *lack of* originality in other art works. The Venus of Medici, for instance, is not comparable to his painting because it is composed of "restorations"; and the Apollo too is unworthy because it is only a "copy." But the force of the stranger's argument suddenly becomes diminished the moment he introduces Socrates' reflection on art. For if the block of marble already contains the statue (which means, metaphorically, that all art is found in the raw material that goes into making it), where does that leave the "originality" of the stranger's painting? Indeed, no originality in art is possible according to the stranger's statement, not even in a painting whose name signifies the origin (Madonna=mother). And the remark that Michael Angelo "was by no means original in his couplet"—implying that Socrates *was* original—must therefore be seen as an ironic comment on originality in general.[16]

Originality is also thrown into question by the stranger's full-length por-

15. Stuart Levine and Susan Levine, *Poe's Short Fiction*, p. 496, cite this translation by Eric Carlson.

16. The irony of this passage is also played out on the level of Poe and Byron, given that we accept Benton's claim that Apollo is a reference to Byron (who Byron's biographer Thomas Moore said resembled the Belvedere Apollo). By calling Apollo (Byron) a copy, Poe seems to be asserting his own originality over his literary father. Of course Poe's is a desire for mastery, for self-presence, which is undermined by the very fact that Poe speaks *through* the Byron figure (the stranger) and *through* (according to Benton's article) Byron's Folingo letter, on which the entire passage is based. In this sense Poe becomes a figure as covered up as Byron, as each can be "seen" only through the other.

It is also worth noting that the opposition between the sun and the artificial light emanating from the stranger's apartment—an opposition alluded to in the second half of the narrative—may also dramatize the struggle for mastery that goes on between the original (natural light) and its imitation or copy (artificial light). That the "gaudy lamps and censors are so eager to subdue" the "solemn sun" (165) is a suggestion that art(ifice) will ultimately replace nature. But, it should be noted, perhaps such a distinction between art and nature is too schematic for such a story as this, where Byron-Apollo (the *sun-god*) becomes the chief dispenser of artificial light (since it is from the stranger's, or "Byron's," apartment that the light comes); in other words, the sun sends out *false* light. All of which seems to suggest that the second half of Poe's narrative does not allow any more access to the stranger than does the first half, no matter how much "light" is cast on the scene.

trait of the Marchesa Aphrodite. Unveiling the portrait to the narrator, the stranger supposedly *reveals* the Marchesa in all her "superhuman beauty." To the narrator, the beautiful woman suddenly comes alive—she is made *present*—since, as he points out, "The same ethereal figure which stood before me the preceding night upon the steps of the Ducal Palace, stood before me once again" (164). Her essence, or original self, is presented—or rather re-presented—in the stranger's illustrious portrait. But such a notion can be looked on only with a certain degree of irony once we realize that the stranger's representation (portrait) of the Marchesa is a representation *of* a representation. For as we recall, the "real" Marchesa is described in relation to an art work—she is "statue-like," with a "marble countenance." Even her gauze-like drapery hangs around her delicate form like "the heavy marble hangs around the Niobe" (153). Indeed, she is the very statue of the Greek goddess after whom she is named. In this sense the stranger's portrait of her serves only to represent something that is absent, that is, the real Marchesa; and so by the logic of Poe's text the portrait *cannot* make her self present—it cannot offer a truth about her.

A similar kind of irony develops in the final scene of "The Assignation." Since both the stranger and the Marchesa (who are mirror images) are already portrayed as art objects—which also means that they are already dead (stone-dead)[17]—the death of the lovers at the end of the story is simply repetition, thus making ironic the idea that they at last, in the final scene, return to an originary state. In "The Assignation," life is a death-in-art, a kind of representation that prevents the discovery of that life's essence.[18] That this representation seems always to be a kind of *cover-up*— a way of concealing truth—becomes especially evident when we examine the particular way in which the narrator calls up the stranger's life.

The narrator's (hi)story of the stranger is a portrait of a life as it "*shouldst be*": how he remembers the stranger in all his essence. Told from the perspective of the present, the narrative aims to recapture a past event, even though the narrator admits that it is "with a confused recollection that I bring to mind the circumstances of that meeting [with the stranger]" (151).

17. The Marchesa's death-like state is equated with her statue-like appearance—a condition that seems to come to a halt once her child is rescued: "Yes! tears are gathering in those eyes— and see! the entire woman thrills throughout the soul, and the statue has started into life!" (154).

18. This relationship between death and representation follows closely on what Derrida, *Of Grammatology*, p. 184, speaks of in regard to the image: "The image is death. A proposition that one may define or make indefinite thus: the image is *a* death or (the) death is *an* image. Imagination is the power that allows life to affect itself within its own re-presentation. The image cannot represent and add the representer to the represented, except in so far as the presence of the represented is already folded back upon itself in the world, in so far as life refers to itself as to its own lack, to its own wish for a supplement. The presence of the represented is constituted with the help of the addition to itself of that nothing which is the image, announcement of its dispossession within its own representer and within its death."

At first unsure as to the exact circumstances of the event—for instance, he is not certain whether it is the third or fourth time he met the person about whom he speaks—the narrator quickly attempts to restore the reader's confidence with the words, "Yet I remember—ah! how should I forget?—the deep midnight, the Bridge of Sighs, the beauty of woman, and the Genius of Romance that stalked up and down the narrow canal" (151). But the faithfulness of his recollection may well be determined by the way in which memory in "The Assignation" is understood. It is in the narrator's physical description of the stranger that the problem of memory—and of remembering the stranger—is brought to our attention in a specific way. Trying to explain the particular mystery that pervades the stranger's person, he recounts his face:

. . . his countenance was, nevertheless, one of those which all men have seen at some period of their lives, and have never afterwards seen again. It had no peculiar—it had no settled predominant expression to be fastened upon the memory; a countenance seen and instantly forgotten—but forgotten with a vague and never-ceasing desire of recalling it to mind. Not that the spirit of each rapid passion failed, at any time, to throw its own distinct image upon the mirror of that face—but that the mirror, mirror-like, retained no vestige of the passion, when the passion had departed. (156)

The narrator's statement that the stranger's countenance is one that all have seen at some time but "have never afterwards seen again" could be interpreted to mean that the stranger possesses an especially unique face, one that is rarely encountered; but given the rest of the passage, the statement also seems to call attention to the way in which the face elicits a certain kind of forgetfulness, so that it becomes a face that, in not being "seen again," is not *remembered*. The face, having no fixed ("settled") expression, vanishes from the mind's eye without a trace and so has to be recalled by way of a "vague and never-ceasing desire." In other words, once forgotten (or covered over), the stranger's face must be reinterpreted. Here the idea of reinterpreting does not mean capturing the truth of that face, as if it possessed some historic identity, but rather laying over with each gesture of interpretation a new "truth" so that the face, instead of remaining a stable entity, becomes something that is forever changing. The moment one engages in the act of seeing/interpreting, as Nietzsche points out, one alters the object of interpretation.[19] The "passion"—or life-essence—reflected (mirrored) in the stranger's face disappears as each "rapid" passion departs, leaving an absence to be filled by a different interpretation,

19. See Friedrich Nietzsche, *The Will to Power*, p. 301: "There are no 'facts-in-themselves,' for a sense must always be projected into them before there can be 'facts.'"

by that "never-ceasing desire of recalling it [the stranger's face] to mind."
Thus forgetting becomes a kind of inventing, a way of covering up the past
so that all "remembered" events are actually invented events. The narrator, this means, does not portray the stranger as he actually *was*—he does
not recover the stranger's life. Rather he recreates the stranger through his
own imagination.

With such a radical notion of memory—whereby remembering is a kind
of forgetting, or a covering over, of "truth" (totalized history) by way of
invention—the authenticity of the narrator's story becomes suspect. The
narrator is not so much remembering as he is forgetting what happened
on his visit to the stranger in Venice. That is, his representation of the
events he recounts is really nothing other than a fictionalization (a covering up)—not a recapturing of events. The narrator's reassurance to the
reader that he *remembers* ("ah! how should I forget?") thus becomes a case
of pure bravado, a defense against the burden of forgetting. His earlier
apostrophe to the stranger is perhaps more to the point: "Again *in fancy* I
behold thee!" (150, emphasis mine).[20]

Of course, since the narrator is included in his own narration, his life
also becomes subjected to the fate of forgetting (a covering up of his own
identity that is dramatized in his remaining, like the stranger, nameless).
For in representing himself, the narrator becomes something other than
who he "is"; he loses his presence and becomes no less a stranger to himself than the stranger. In fact, we may say that he recreates himself in
the image of the stranger, identifying with him in such a way as to be the
stranger's double, or mirror image. Like the stranger, the narrator "lives" a
kind of death-in-art. Describing the stranger's death at the end of the story,
the narrator reports that "his limbs were rigid—his lips were livid—his
lately beaming eyes were riveted in *death*" (166). Earlier on, the narrator
described himself in similar terms. Here he is caught up in the scene of the
drowning child near the Bridge of Sighs:

Stupefied and aghast, I had myself no power to move from the upright position I
had assumed upon first hearing the [Marchesa's] shriek, and must have presented
to the eyes of the agitated group a spectral and ominous appearance, as with pale

20. That the narrator becomes something of a visionary, a man of imagination, associates
him closely with the visionary-stranger and thus puts in question many of those analyses that
attempt to see the two characters as representing a split between imagination/vision and
rationality. Specifically I refer to George H. Soule, Jr., "Byronism in Poe's 'Metzengerstein'
and 'William Wilson,'" who reads "The Assignation" as "another satire on the bifurcated
Byronic personality"—a reading that depends on seeing the narrator as the symbol of
rationality and the stranger as the symbol of irrational passions. Edward Pitcher, "Poe's 'The
Assignation': A Reconsideration," contends: "The narrator does not *see* what the artist/
visionary sees." Though Pitcher does point out that there develops a "complex balancing of
what each [of the characters] represents," he fails to see that both are bound up in each other's
"identity" from the beginning.

countenance and rigid limbs, I floated down among them in that funereal gondola. (153)

Seen in conjunction with his "spectral and ominous appearance," his "pale countenance," and the "funereal gondola" in which he travels, the narrator's "rigid limbs"—like those of the stranger in the final scene—connote death. That the narrator also finds himself frozen in an "upright position" connects him (rhetorically) with the lines from Chapman's *Bussy d'Ambois* ("He is up / There like a Roman statue! He will stand / Till Death hath made him marble!") and thus calls attention to his *own* death-in-art. To be sure, the narrator is no less a work of art, a representation, than the stranger and the Marchesa.[21] It seems as if, unable to stand outside the scene of the story, the narrator must lose his own "life" in the art (or story) he is creating; and in the process of becoming a representation he must lose a certain mastery over the lives and events he is supposed to recover. This is perhaps dramatized in the fact that when he enters the scene near the Bridge of Sighs—which seems to parallel his entrance into the (hi)story of the stranger—he loses that sign of control, his oar, "in the pitchy darkness beyond a chance of recovery" (151–52). Once inside the scene of the story (and we must recognize that he is always already there, since his narration begins with his very first words, "Ill-fated and mysterious man!" [150]), the narrator cannot stand outside. He cannot attain mastery over, or a privileged position in relation to, the text.

We can say that the narrator's difficulty in recovering the "life" of the stranger (the alleged purpose of his narrative) amounts to nothing less than his own difficulty in recovering himself—his own mirror image. As we have already mentioned, such a difficulty in locating/seeing/recovering the original self (one's essence) stems precisely from the *act of representing*, which, always being a kind of interpretation, a reading, cannot help but reinvent—and thus cover up—the "true self." In this sense the "real" Byron remains an elusive figure, covered up in Poe's story's interpretation of the Byron legend (which is itself perpetuated by other texts that Poe's story interprets and, in the process, disfigures[22]). This does not really contradict Benton's—and others'—claims that "The Assignation" is a hoax as much as it complicates their reasons for calling it such. For if Byron *is* present in the story as a primary influence, which is the main line of Benton's argument, then we must understand *influence* here not as a unified identity that stands behind, and originates, the work but rather as what Harold Bloom refers to as a "relation between texts" (in which case we must

21. It should also be mentioned, in connection with the death-like state of the characters, that Mentoni is described similarly, as he "seemed *ennuyé* to the very death" (153).

22. Benton, "Poe's 'The Assignation,'" pp. 194–95, points out that much of Poe's knowledge of Byron's life, as it is filtered through "The Assignation," comes from his reading of Thomas Moore's *Letters and Journals of Lord Byron, with Notices of His Life* (London: J. Murray, 1830).

regard "The Assignation" as Poe's *reading* of Byron).[23] What is especially interesting is the way Poe's story dramatizes—and plays with—the problem of *influence*. An example of this comes in connection with the English poem that the narrator stumbles upon and suspects is the stranger's.

Though the story leaves a trail of evidence to suggest that the poem was indeed written by the stranger, it likewise attempts to cover up that trail. We notice, first, the narrator's remark that the poem is "written in a hand so very different from the peculiar characters of my acquaintance [the stranger], that I had some difficulty in recognising it as his own" (162) and, second, that some of the leading evidence as to the author's identity is discredited by "a report involving so many improbabilities" (164). That the *origin* (authorship, source) of this poem becomes problematic is further accentuated by the fact that the poem's place of date—where the poem *comes from*—"had been originally *London*, and afterwards carefully overscored" (163). It is precisely this surrounding problem of originality that Poe plays with in his reading, and concealing, of Byron. The poem, though apparently ascribed to the Byron figure of the story (the stranger), is actually one of Poe's own poems he published previously—and separately from "The Assignation"—under the title "To Ianthe in Heaven."[24] The insertion of this poem thus becomes a ploy on Poe's part to reinterpret, if not reinvent, Byron in Poe's own image. Indeed Byron becomes "present" only insofar as he speaks *through* Poe. But, of course, the irony that prevents us from ever determining *who* is actually speaking here—who is the true author (and origin) of the poem—is provided by what Poe's source-hunters have already pointed out: Poe's "own" poem is one that carries with it the "hint of Byronism," with its employment of typical Byronic images (such as "thunder-blasted tree," "green isle," and "fountain and a shrine").[25] In this case, we must now see Poe as speaking *through* Byron.

But should we believe that the intertextual nature of "The Assignation" ends with the uncanny literary relationship shown to exist between Poe

23. In Bloom's revisionist poetics, the writer is always seeking out strategies to confront or evade previous "father" texts. The writer's relation with his predecessor (his origins) is always antithetical. The view that affirms the position of the poet/writer as self-possessed creator of meaning is one that Bloom dismisses. Harold Bloom, *A Map of Misreading*, p. 3, argues: "Influence, as I conceive it, means that there are *no* texts, but only relationships *between* texts. These relationships depend upon a critical act, a misreading or misprision, that one poet performs upon another, and that does not differ in kind from the necessary critical acts performed by every strong reader upon every text he encounters. The influence-relation governs reading as it governs writing, and reading is therefore a miswriting just as writing is a misreading." Though Bloom's revisionism is informing for my reading of Poe, I agree with Bloom only up to a point. His reinstitution of the author's personality and presence is finally at variance with my reading.

24. Poe printed the poem as "To Ianthe in Heaven," in July 1839 in *Gentleman's Magazine*. As part of the story the poem is generally referred to as "To One in Paradise."

25. Basler, "Byronism," pp. 232–36, discusses in detail the many Byronic images that Poe employs in the story's poem.

and Byron, we need only consider the story's relationship to an earlier version of "The Assignation" entitled "The Visionary." In *reading* "The Visionary," "The Assignation" in a way covers up Poe's earlier text by omitting certain passages. That it should omit, in particular, the *beginning* paragraphs of "The Visionary" perhaps comes as no surprise, given the sort of conscious attention Poe's story pays to the problem of representation: for it is in the act of representation, of reading, of revision, that origins are canceled. We can thus say that "The Assignation" enacts the kind of covering up that reading implies. But here the questions must be posed: What does the "original" text offer in the way of truth? What do the beginning paragraphs reveal? Following is the text of those paragraphs as they first appeared in *Godey's Lady's Book* in January 1834:

There is a name—a sound—which, above all other music, vibrates upon my ear with a delicious, yet wild and solemn melody. Devoutly admired by the few who read, and by the very few who think, it is a name not as yet, indeed, blazoned in the escutcheon of immortality; but there, nevertheless, heralded in characters of that Tyrian fire hereafter to be rendered legible by the breath of centuries.

It is a name, moreover, which for reasons intrinsically of no weight, yet in fact conclusive, I am determined to conceal. Nor will I, by fictitious appellation, dishonor the memory of that great dead whose life was so little understood, and the received account of whose melancholy end is a tissue of malevolent blasphemies. I am not of that class of writers who, making some euphonous cognomen the keystone to the arch of their narrations, can no more conclude without the one than the architect without the other.[26]

We discover that the passage speaks directly to the problem of covering up the identity of the figure around whom the story revolves; and through its various metaphors, the passage suggests the way in which that "covering-up" operates. There is a suspicion from the first sentence that the name of the stranger might summon up too ethereal an order to allow it to be debased by verbal language; it is perhaps too musical for words (and so should not even be named a name, but a "sound"). But the narrator's language soon reveals that words, especially written words, are unavoidable in making "present" the stranger, since the stranger's name (which becomes associated with his life) will be "heralded in *characters* of that Tyrian fire hereafter to be rendered *legible* by the breath of centuries" (emphases mine). The references to writing decidedly point out that the stranger can be "seen" in no other way than through words. We might possibly assume from this that the narrator is being somewhat self-regarding, suggesting that it is precisely through the language of *his* story that the stranger will "live."

26. Benjamin Franklin Fisher IV, "To 'The Assignation' from 'The Visionary' and Poe's Decade of Revising," p. 90, has incorporated into his commentary the full text of "The Visionary" as it first appeared in 1834.

That this "life" can exist only as being covered up in language becomes even more evident once we examine the implications of the second paragraph. Here, in his reluctance to name the stranger—even with a "fictitious appellation"—the narrator compares himself to an architect (even if it is only to show what kind of architect he is not). The association he makes between narrating/writing and architecture helps to put into perspective our understanding of the stranger's position in the story: the stranger's first "appearance"—in the shadows of the prison's architecture—might now be interpreted to mean that he is imprisoned (covered up) in language itself—and more specifically, in the language of Poe's text. To be sure, it is his representation *in writing* that subverts his self-presence.[27]

Of course each new reading, each new re-vision of "The Visionary" (and of the stranger, to whom the title refers), becomes another architectural structure superimposed on the last, further concealing the stranger's identity, his (hi)story. Thus, it would seem, any attempt to recover the stranger, whether it be made by Poe (in "The Assignation") or by the many commentators on the story, can only result in a *re-covering*. To name Byron as the figure who stands behind "The Assignation" is, in this sense, to repeat the kind of covering up that the story already enacts.

Why Poe chooses Byron as a vehicle to explore questions of selfhood and self-presence is perhaps related to the general nineteenth-century view of the English poet as an emblem of the romantic ideal. Poe himself, as biographers point out, was obsessed with cultivating a Byronic stance, trying to identify with the poet in every way. In his youth he swam six miles down the James River, as Byron had swum the Hellespont, and wrote verses in a Byronic mode. While attending the University of Virginia in 1826, as George Soule notes, "he maintained the pose, drinking, gambling, reading poetry and tales in his rooms, and drawing charcoal sketches of the plates from a Byron edition on the walls."[28] Poe continued to be influenced by Byron throughout his life. "The Assignation" is instructive because it dramatizes how Poe's identity is bound up in Byron's,

---

27. In some ways Poe anticipates the work of the French literary critic Maurice Blanchot, who has made an extensive examination of the way in which the self loses itself—is annihilated—in language. In *The Gaze of Orpheus*, trans. Lydia Davis, p. 42, for example, Blanchot writes: "A word may give me its meaning, but first it suppresses it. For me to be able to say, 'This woman' I must somehow take her flesh and blood reality away from her, cause her to be absent, annihilate her. The word gives me the being, but it gives it to me deprived of being. The word is the absence of that being, its nothingness, what is left of it when it has lost being—the very fact that it does not exist." For an elaborate discussion on the way writing upsets self-presence, see Derrida, *Of Grammatology*: "Writing is that forgetting of the self, that exteriorization, the contrary of the interiorizing memory" (p. 24); writing is, moreover, "the dissimulation of the natural, primary, and immediate presence of sense to the soul within the logos" (p. 37).

28. Soule, "Byronism," p. 152. See also Arthur H. Quinn, *Edgar Allan Poe: A Critical Biography*.

in effect how Byron becomes that interpretive fiction into which Poe reads himself.[29] Byron stands as Poe's other, an other from which *Poe's* "identity" cannot extricate itself so as to be fully present to itself. What "The Assignation" accomplishes, finally, is to ironize in advance the romantic quest for origins, for truth, for presence—the quest that critics implicitly affirm when they produce Byron as the text's ultimate referent.

29. I refer to Poe not as a historic identity, total and present to itself, but as an interpretive fiction, in other words, as the series of texts that are attached to that name. In this sense, Poe's revision of his own writing, the writing that is a *reading* of Byron, is also a reading of himself.

3 POE/SCRIPT
The Death of the Author in
The Narrative of Arthur Gordon Pym

The Narrative of Arthur Gordon Pym is a text riddled with mysteries, not the least of which involves Pym's seeming annihilation at the story's end:

And now we rushed into the embraces of the cataract, where a chasm threw itself open to receive us [Pym and Dirk Peters]. But there arose in our pathway a shrouded human figure, very far larger in its proportions than any dweller among men. And the hue of the skin of the figure was of the perfect whiteness of the snow.[1]

Most of the commentary on this passage centers exclusively on the meaning of the "shrouded human figure" and the "perfect whiteness" into which Pym voyages, all to bring a sense of closure, of determinacy, to what is represented as an open-ended text.[2] Unsatisfied with the abrupt ending of Pym's *Narrative*—an ending that leaves much to be answered regarding the hero's fate—critics have attempted to close the gap in Poe's text with a kind of symbolizing that, depending on the theoretical orientation, has either religious or psychoanalytic implications. Edward H. Davidson, for instance, argues that the whiteness at the end of Pym's journey signals the culmination of Pym's ever increasing moral and spiritual awareness; indeed "the blankness of eternal mystery engulfs him the moment he faces the white light of revelation."[3] Offering a Freudian interpretation, Marie Bonaparte reads the final scene as symbolic of Pym's return to the womb, with the "perfect whiteness" of the human figure representing the mother's milk.[4] Both these readings point out that Pym's death coincides precisely with his greatest self-discovery, or his discovery of his true self (from the psychoanalytic viewpoint, Pym is returning to his origins): his death is a rebirth.

But in attempting to locate the meaning of the white mist that Pym encounters, critics have in a sense repeated Pym's quest for ultimate truth

1. Edgar Allan Poe, *The Narrative of Arthur Gordon Pym*, in *Collected Writings of Edgar Allan Poe*, ed. Burton R. Pollin, 1:206. All future references to *Pym* pertain to this edition.
2. The "open-endedness" of the text refers to the way in which the narrative abruptly breaks off without our knowing what happens to Pym. The unnamed author of the Note informs us of the loss of two or three final chapters of the text.
3. Edward H. Davidson, *Poe: A Critical Study*, p. 177.
4. Marie Bonaparte, *The Life and Works of Edgar Allan Poe: A Psycho-Analytic Interpretation*, trans. John Rodker, p. 351.

and knowledge. Not that the critic must fall to the same disastrous fate as Pym, but whatever "knowledge" he comes upon must necessarily prove fruitless, impossible to possess. Poe may well anticipate his readers—his decipherers—insofar as his text, by creating a gap or space into which (let us say) the reader must voyage, makes ironic the very idea of bringing the text to a successful closure, with a correct meaning. For the "white light of revelation" is really no revelation at all; it simply marks the absence around which the reader is allowed to construct his own interpretive discourse, filling in the blank space with his own sort of fiction. What Poe's text accomplishes here is not to represent an ultimate knowledge of the self but rather to establish the conditions on which such a knowledge is possible: thus to show how "truth"—and more specifically, the truth of the self— is not discovered, but invented. In *The Narrative of Arthur Gordon Pym,* Poe challenges whatever authenticity, or truth-value, the narrator might lend to his narrative by putting in question the narrator's self—that is, his ability to stand outside his own system of representation, total and present to himself. We have seen already how "The Fall of the House of Usher" and "The Assignation" subject their narrators to their own particular textual (or interpretive) estrangement, but such a problematic may be said to culminate in *Pym,* as here the *author himself* becomes the chief vehicle through which Poe explores questions of selfhood and self-presence. What precisely *is* authorship? And how, at the same time that it is supposed to authenticate a given text, does it jeopardize its own authority?

It is perhaps in the final scene of *Pym* that the problem of authorship— and hence of the authenticity of the entire text—becomes most transparent; for here we confront the paradoxical situation of an author seemingly narrating his own demise. That the story may be a hoax in this respect has become the opinion of more than a few critics;[5] but Poe's concern with the problem of authorship becomes too insistent throughout the text for us to reduce the story to a mere hoax—and so we would perhaps do better to see Pym's death as a dramatization of this problem. We may well relate Poe's investigation of "the author" to Michel Foucault's explanation of the relationship that exists between writing and death. In his essay "What is an Author?" Foucault, discussing our modern culture, argues:

Writing has become linked to sacrifice, even to the sacrifices of life: it is now a voluntary effacement which does not need to be represented in books, since it is brought about in the writer's very existence. . . . That is not all, however: this relationship between writing and death is also manifested in the effacement of the writing subject's individual characteristics. Using all the contrivances that he sets up between himself and what he writes, the writing subject cancels out the signs of

5. For discussions of hoaxing in Poe, see G. R. Thompson, *Poe's Fiction: Romantic Irony in the Gothic Tales,* and Daniel Hoffman, *Poe Poe Poe Poe Poe Poe Poe.*

his particular individuality. As a result, the mark of the writer is reduced to nothing more than the singularity of his absence; he must assume the role of the dead man in the game of writing.[6]

That Pym's death at the story's end may be related to his disappearance in writing—to the death of the author—becomes more plausible once we realize that "narrative authority" is set forth as a problem from the very beginning of Poe's text, in the preface. Here Poe raises the question of authorship by going so far as to call attention to *his own* activity of writing a work of fiction; that is, he names himself as the fictional author-character, "Mr. Poe, lately editor of the Southern Literary Messenger" (55), who also shares in the writing of Pym's *Narrative*. Inscribing himself in the scene of his own writing, Poe thus dramatizes his own disappearance, his "death," in writing; he subverts his own self-presence. Who, then, can be said to author the text if no clear demarcation exists between the writer and the written? And if "author" at once implies the origin of the work, who then stands *before* the text, originating and authorizing it?

Such questions are implicitly posed by the preface. Here Pym claims to have entrusted the task of writing part of the narrative to Mr. Poe, mainly because he lacks the confidence in his own writing to convince very many readers that the "marvelous" events he wishes to report are true. Drawing up, "in his own words, a narrative of the earlier portion of my [Pym's] adventures," Poe publishes it in the Southern Messenger, "*under the garb of fiction*" (56). Ironically, the fiction is taken by the public as fact, and Pym decides thereupon to complete the narrative that Poe began, believing now that "the facts of my narrative would prove of such a nature as to carry with them sufficient evidence of their own authenticity" (56).

A problem of authorship arises, however, when we try to distinguish between Poe's portion of the narrative and Pym's. Though Pym, in the last lines of the preface, assures us that "the difference in point of style will be readily perceived" (56), there seems to be no detectable change in style throughout the narrative, thus preventing any attempt to reach a clear understanding of who is writing when, or who the real author is. It is true, as several critics have noted, that Pym is a sort of double of Poe, his name even being reminiscent of Poe's.[7] But the doubling of Poe and Pym is more than a simple hoax, a game that Poe is playing with his readers; it serves as a point of departure for the text's exploration into the meaning of authorship and into the consequences that writing holds for any epistemological pursuits, that is, for any search for truth and knowledge. For Pym's jour-

6. Michel Foucault, "What is an Author?" in *Textual Strategies: Perspectives in Post-Structuralist Criticism*, ed. Josue V. Harari, pp. 142-43.
7. For a discussion of the doubling of Poe and Pym, see Harold Beaver, Introduction to *The Narrative of Arthur Gordon Pym* (New York: Penguin Books, 1960), p. 9.

ney, as we learn, is as much a verbal one as it is a physical one; and it should therefore not be surprising that his whole movement toward origins, truth, presence—what Davidson calls the "white light of revelation"—is undermined by the very fact of his authorship.

The entire structure of *Pym* may be said to indicate a movement toward origins, as the hero's journey seems to take him not only to the source of himself—as already suggested by Marie Bonaparte's analysis of the womb motif—but also to the corresponding beginnings of man: among a tribe of islanders too geographically isolated to be corrupted by civilization. At the island of Tsalal, near the South Pole, Pym fulfills his earlier romantic visions of traveling to "some gray and desolate rock, in an ocean unapproachable and unknown" (65). Here, far from the conventional world of his New England home, Pym encounters "nature" itself—that realm that appears to be free from what Melville will later refer to as the "world of lies." Pym's seeming quest for truth and knowledge, for a certain essentiality in life, is apparently fulfilled by this pure, natural, unblemished landscape. It is a veritable heart of darkness into which Pym enters, where man is reduced to his most primitive state. Thus the "savages" found here are described as "about the ordinary stature of Europeans, but of a more muscular and brawny frame, their complexion a jet black, with thick and long woolly hair. They were clothed in skins of an unknown black animal, shaggy and silky" (168).

A literally uncultured people, the tribesmen of Tsalal are represented as being prelinguistic; the sounds they utter—such as *Anamoo-moo!* and *Lama-Lama!* (174) and other such cries—resemble what Marie Bonaparte has insightfully identified as "infant babble."[8] To be sure, infants, according to romantic doctrine, are closely associated with the natural. But if Poe's text does not provide enough evidence to confirm that the Tsalalians' speech derives from the mouths of babes, there are more explicit suggestions that their form of communication comes precisely from nature itself. For instance, when the Tsalalians confront anything that is colored white—such as the white carcass of "the strange animal with the scarlet teeth and claws" (190)—they begin shouting *Tekeli-li!* (190), a sound that we later discover is likewise produced by the "gigantic and pallidly white birds" (205-6) that issue from the vapory white curtain Pym encounters in the final scene. Also, when the captive islander Nu-Nu speaks the names *Tsalal* and *Tsalemon*, which designate the island and the island king respectively, he makes "a prolonged hissing sound . . . which was precisely the same with the note of the black bittern we [Pym and his party] had eaten upon the summit of the hill" (204).

Dominated by the "voice" of nature, the world of Tsalal must be said to

8. Bonaparte, *Edgar Allan Poe*, p. 338.

exist outside of language altogether, in a realm that is uncorrupted by another of man's "lies," or artifices. According to Saussurian linguistics, language is constituted only within a system of differences, and identity can be formulated only in terms of difference.[9] But on the island of Tsalal, which seems to elude the conventions of language, we witness a society immersed in *sameness*—where the uniform appearance of the island and its inhabitants allows for few distinctions. Complementing a region further along in Pym's journey, where nothing that is *not* white is to be found, Tsalal is represented as predominantly black. The complexions of the islanders, as already mentioned, are "jet black" (168); the domestic animals include hog-like creatures with black wool, and even a black albatross (173); the islanders known as *Wampoos* live in "black skin palaces" (174); even the teeth of these islanders are black (205); and finally, the island itself consists of black granite (194).

One incident that is particularly revealing about the Tsalalians' sense of self-sameness occurs aboard the *Jane Guy*, with the schooner's arrival at the island. The island chief, who decides to inspect the vessel (which he takes to be a living creature), happens on his "reflected self" in the cabin mirrors and nearly dies from fright (169). Obviously, the scene points to a society of people so removed from civilization as not to have experienced anything as unnatural as a mirror. Yet the scene also carries the implication that in this pure, self-contained society one does not locate one's identity in relation to his essential otherness, as in Lacanian psychoanalysis,[10] but rather one is complete *in himself,* in other words, is self-identical. The order of the other in the formation of one's identity is completely absent in this world that is outside the differential structure of language.

Of course Pym's journey into this originary landscape is nothing less than a reflection of the hero's own psychic movement toward his true, natural self. As Davidson argues, the events of Pym's journey are "an external mirroring of his own mind."[11] But there is another way in which the text dramatizes Pym's gradual confrontation with himself, and that is through the sort of doubling of selves that is so familiar to Poe's fiction. For Pym's successive associations with his New England schoolmate, Augustus Barnard, and with Dirk Peters, the half-breed Indian whom he befriends while on board the *Grampus,* in a way define his romantic quest for origins.

The identification between Pym and Augustus is made early in the nar-

9. See Ferdinand de Saussure, *Course in General Linguistics*, trans. Wade Baskin. See also Jonathan Culler, *Ferdinand de Saussure*, p. 72: "Meaning depends on difference of meaning; only through difference of meaning can one identify forms and their defining functional qualities. Forms are not something given; they must be established through analysis of a system of relations and differences."

10. See Jacques Lacan, "The Mirror-phase as Formative of the Function of the I," trans. Jean Roussel.

11. Davidson, *Poe*, p. 173.

rative, when they are shown to be inseparable companions—to the point of
sometimes occupying the same bed at night (57). It may of course be possible to draw homoerotic implications from such an association,[12] but the
real emphasis of their relationship—as psychological doubles, as opposed
to sexual partners—becomes clearer in Pym's statement concerning the
kind of influence that Augustus's sea stories have on him: "Augustus thoroughly entered into my state of mind. It is probable, indeed, that our intimate communion had resulted in a partial *interchange of character*" (65,
emphasis mine). Augustus, whose name, as Daniel Hoffman points out,
is associated "with both the Age of Reason and with C. Auguste Dupin,"[13]
apparently represents that side of Pym that is rationalistic; indeed we
observe Augustus's calculating mind when he cleverly arranges Pym's
escape to sea on board his father's whaling vessel, the *Grampus*.

Pym's handsome, white, Anglo-Saxon counterpart, whose eloquent
manner of speaking incites Pym's wanderlust, is in direct contrast to Pym's
more ferocious-looking and enigmatic double, Dirk Peters. Peters, who
comes to replace Augustus as Pym's most intimate companion—and does
so completely when Augustus dies—appears more animal-like than
human, with legs that "were *bowed* in the most singular manner, and
appeared to possess no flexibility whatever" (87). With an immense bald
head on which he wears a bearskin wig, and with long, protruding teeth,
Peters represents Pym's dark, savage self. Though it may be true, as Leslie
Fiedler asserts, that Peters's grotesque appearance reflects Poe's own aris-
tocratic, and finally racist, attitude toward Indians and blacks in America,
it would seem more in keeping with Poe's emphasis on metaphysical matters to see Peters primarily as an emblem of the deep, mysterious truth of
Pym's being—that point of "nature" that Pym must approach within himself finally to know who he is.[14]

But as already suggested, Pym's movement toward an originary state—
his true self—seems to imply a simultaneous death (as such a movement
does in the culmination of his journey from the conventional world of New
England to the primitive setting of the South Seas). In his movement from
his Augustus-self to his Peters-self, Pym experiences a similar coincidence
between death and his confrontation with his origins, depicted most poi-
gnantly in the scene in which Pym and Peters attempt to escape from their
desperate conditions on the island of Tsalal. Climbing down a sheer cliff
wall, Pym stares "far down into the abyss" and is suddenly overcome with
"*a longing to fall*" (198). It is an episode in some ways reminiscent of the final

12. For a discussion of the homoerotic implications in *Pym*, see Leslie Fiedler, *Love and Death
in the American Novel*, pp. 391–400.
13. Hoffman, *Poe Poe*, p. 269.
14. Fiedler, *Love and Death*, p. 397.

scene, in which Pym seems to perish in the embraces of the cataract. But instead of the "perfect whiteness," standing ready to receive Pym in this instance is the dark figure of Dirk Peters:

> I let go at once my grasp upon the peg, and, turning half round from the precipice, remained tottering for an instant against its naked face. But now there came a spinning of the brain; a shrill-sounding and phantom voice screamed within my ears; a dusky, fiendish, and filmy figure stood immediately beneath me; and, sighing, I sunk down with a bursting heart, and plunged within its arms. (198)

Peters becomes—like the cataract—a kind of womb into which Pym falls, and thus his maternal embrace would seem to suggest for Pym a return to origins.[15] That Pym endures a death-into-life is confirmed further on, when Pym reports that after his being saved by Peters, "animation returned" and he felt himself "a new being" (198). To be sure, death is linked once again with Pym's seeming movement toward an originary state, toward his becoming one with the true self, as represented here by Peters.

   Though the general movement of Pym's journey is toward an originary (or natural) state—where Pym can finally locate the truth of himself—such a movement, we must now observe, is suddenly undermined by the fact that Pym finds himself caught in a completely textual environment. From the preface we understand that Pym may well be a product of Mr. Poe's imagination, as Mr. Poe is said to have coauthored the narrative (though just how much of it remains uncertain). This idea is further suggested when we discover, early in the narrative, that Pym's origin—the starting point of his journey/narrative—is a place called *Edgar*ton, as if to imply that Mr. [Edgar] Poe is Pym's true beginning, his origin, his author. (Though it is true that Edgarton is an actual town in New England, it is reasonable to assume that it becomes here a sly allusion to "Mr. Poe" of the preface, who stands as Pym's double.) Indeed, we can see that Pym's authorship is from the start problematic, that aside from posing as a writing self he also finds himself in the position of a *written self*.[16] Are we to assume, since the real Poe subverts his own authorship by portraying himself as a fictional character (in the preface), that even Pym's "origin" is subject to a certain textual displacement—that it is a fiction?

15. Ibid., p. 396. Fiedler's inclination to read the passage as a sexual fantasy leads him to say that "the studied ambiguity of the passage, in which the language of horror becomes that of eroticism, the dying plunge becomes a climactic embrace, makes it clear that the *longing to fall* and the desire for the dark spouse are one, a single perverseness."

16. For a thorough discussion of the way in which the writing self becomes the written self, see John T. Irwin, *American Hieroglyphics: The Symbol of the Egyptian Hieroglyphics in the American Renaissance*, pp. 114–29.

There are several indications that Pym's whole sea adventure—or his adventurer-self—has its "origin" in storytelling of one form or another. It is Augustus's "stories of the natives of the Island of Tinian, and other places he had visited in his travels" that first whet Pym's appetite for adventure and that eventually result in his going out in his sailboat, the *Ariel*, on "some of the maddest freaks in the world" (57). Other stories that Pym's boyhood companion relates—half of which Pym suspects are "sheer fabrications"—presage many of Pym's harrowing adventures on board the *Grampus* and the *Jane Guy*. Indeed, Augustus's tales of romance inspire precisely the sort of visions Pym reports later as having experienced: "visions . . . of shipwreck and famine; of death or captivity among barbarian hordes" (65). Even when Pym is sequestered in the bottom of the *Grampus*, he encounters stories that anticipate the very adventures he will soon experience. Here in his "ironbound box" Pym finds among the books left to him one that narrates the "expedition of Lewis and Clarke [*sic*] to the mouth of the Columbia" (70). Such a narrative has particular relevance to Pym's own journey inasmuch as Pym not only will explore hitherto unknown waters—as did the two American explorers—but also will attempt to arrive at a place that designates undiscovered origins (as the more remote parts of the Columbia did for Lewis and Clark, who were trying to locate the Mississippi's most northern source).[17] In a sense, Pym ends up repeating what is already inscribed in a previous text, thus making his "journey toward origins" not in the least original.

Pym's journey, it should be remembered, could not possibly have begun were it not for a forged note. While stowing away on the *Grampus*, Pym excuses his absence from home by having his father receive a note, forged by Augustus, explaining that Pym is invited to spend a fortnight with the sons of a family friend, Mr. Ross. The entire scheme for Pym's escape is completely Augustus's idea, from the time Augustus comes up with the idea to the time he charges himself with "the enditing [*sic*] of this note and getting it delivered" (66); and so once again we see that it is Augustus's "story"—his fiction—that seems to initiate Pym's adventures on the high seas.

Since the "self" that Pym represents has its origins in other fiction—is really a textual self—Pym's "journey toward origins" may be said to mark a desire to escape the confines of fictionality, to become one with himself, to become his own author. But can he really be the author of his own text in the sense of standing *outside* it, in a position of having complete mastery

---

17. Irwin, *American Hieroglyphics*, pp. 77–78, sees the image of the mouth of the Columbia as associated with "a nexus of traditional images of origin that was reworked during the Romantic period, under the pressure of recent historical events." Included in this nexus are the sources of the Nile and of the Mississippi, and the South Pole.

over it? As the preface raises the possibility of a confusion of identities between Pym and Mr. Poe, one is never quite certain who is being written by whom, who is the writing self and who is the written self. In a sense, the rest of the narrative—Pym's journey—plays out this sort of struggle for mastery between the writer and the written, the interpreter and the interpreted, with various surrogate authors (or authority figures) whom Pym must "overthrow" to fulfill his ultimate desire. In this respect we can view the entire journey as an interpretive one, analogous to the very *representation* of that journey in writing. Pym's need to master his physical destiny on the high seas parallels exactly, indeed becomes no different from, his desire to win control over the text by becoming that text's author, its origin.

Throughout the narrative Pym must contend with a number of father figures, the first two being his own father, a sea store trader from Nantucket, and his grandfather, Peterson, a wealthy Edgarton attorney. The example of Peterson is revealing in that Pym, though he is shown to be able to elude the control of his "father," cannot finally come to a position of mastery over himself. In the last instant before he is about to board the ship, Pym escapes his grandfather's notice by disguising himself as a sailor—wearing "a seaman's cloak" and feigning a seaman's gruff manner of speech (67). In other words, to free himself of his "father" and thus to become his own origin (his true self), he must paradoxically become someone other than himself—he must dissimulate. Later on, in an effort to get control of the ship, Pym alarms the superstitious mutineers by disguising himself as the dead crewman, Rogers; that is, he represents himself as the "revivification of his disgusting corpse, or at least its spiritual image" (112). Again, Pym must resort to absenting himself—losing himself in an image or representation—in order to overthrow a certain authority figure. In the process of attaining mastery, Pym loses it.

But Pym need not lose himself in disguise to make ironic whatever control he has over his journey, since with each overthrow of an authority figure there seems to be another authority figure to take his place. Such figures aboard ship include Captain Barnard, the mutineers, Captain Guy, Augustus, and Peters (the name of the last recalling Pym's grandfather, Peterson). Pym in some way tries to supersede all of these "heads" to become the head person himself—the author of his interpretive journey. It is not surprising, therefore, that much of the struggle for mastery that goes on throughout the narrative is depicted in images of *beheadings* (or simply injuries to the head). We see, for instance, Captain Barnard fall victim to the villainous mutineers, sustaining "a deep wound in the forehead, from which blood was flowing in a continued stream" (85). Parker, one of the mutineers who comes into possession of the ship, in turn receives from Pym "a blow on the head" with a pump handle which Pym uses to arm himself (112). And if Pym delivers blows to the head, so too does he receive them, and with a greater frequency. Often Pym's "injuries" to the head involve a mental disability—loss of memory or feelings of delirium due to hunger—but there are as well specific references to physical assaults on the head. For example, Pym finds himself perilously affixed to the bottom of the *Penguin*, where the "head of the bolt had made its way through the collar of the green baize jacket [Pym] had on, and through the back part of [his] neck" (62); and Pym's dog, Tiger, having apparently gone mad, attacks him in his ironbound box, the dog's "sharp teeth pressing vigorously upon the woollen which enveloped [Pym's] neck" (82).

Pym's loss of mastery is perhaps best demonstrated by the fact that some of the authority figures—who also act as guides along his journey—do not by any means lead Pym in a direction of truth but instead call attention to the falsity of interpretation, and to the absence (or death) that interpretation brings to the interpreter.[18] This is seen most clearly in connection with Pym's closest associates, Augustus and Dirk Peters, both of whom "manage" Pym's journey at the same time as they undermine it. Of course Pym's associates could not do otherwise, given that Pym's journey consists of his attempt to become manager/author of his own journey; but the text more explicitly dramatizes Pym's inability to attain the status of manager/author by suggesting that Pym's guides lead him to as much darkness as light, to as much a sense of death as one of life. Augustus is shown to take control of Pym's life at sea when Pym "knew little about the management of a boat" (59); and when Pym pursues his scheme of deception—in order to join the crew of the *Grampus*—he is "obliged to leave much to the management of Augustus" (66). But despite his sense of management, Augustus puts his friend's life in jeopardy by going out in a stormy sea while in a "highly-concentrated state of intoxication" (59) and thus wrecking Pym's sailboat. Arranging Pym's escape on board the *Grampus*, Augustus installs Pym in a coffin-like box, where the latter eventually experiences "the most gloomy imaginings, in which the dreadful deaths of thirst, famine, suffocation, and premature interment, crowded upon me as the prominent disasters to be encountered" (75–76). Indeed, with Augustus as his guide, Pym enters into a realm of darkness, of death.

The hybrid "line-manager" (86) Dirk Peters takes up where Augustus leaves off in managing Pym's affairs, serving at once as the image of security and—because of his physical appearance and his name—as the

18. Simply, this means that the interpreter cannot stand in a privileged position in relation to what he is interpreting, since in the process of interpreting he cannot help but become the very object of interpretation—thus losing himself within the confines of textuality. The writer/interpreter subverts his self-presence in the act of interpreting. Says Eugenio Donato, "The Two Languages of Criticism," in Richard Macksey and Eugenio Donato, *The Structuralist Controversy*, p. 96: "What begins by being the questioning of the subject inevitably turns out to be an indictment of him who questions in the first place."

image of threatening danger.[19] Though he does save Pym from falling off the cliff, we must remember that he is described even in that scene as a "dusky, fiendish, and filmy figure," in other words, as a figure not altogether friendly. As Fiedler points out, "Peters is not made an angelic representative of instinct and nature even at this critical instant; he remains still a fiend, even in the act of becoming a savior."[20] As already mentioned, implied in Pym's plunge into Peters's embrace is a kind of death—a loss of Pym's self the moment he ostensibly finds it. This "death," together with the deathly connotation of Peters's first name (dirk=dagger), indicates exactly what kind of consequences interpretation has for Pym.[21]

It should not go unnoticed that Dirk Peters, though he is a kind of interpreter for Pym, is also directly related to writing/interpretation through his name: a dirk (dagger)—like a writing instrument—cuts, indents, inscribes. Style, it may be remembered, not only means a "mode of expressing thought in language" (*Webster's Seventh New Collegiate Dictionary*) but also may refer to a stylus, which is an instrument used to make imprints or incisions and, in an early usage, is "a weapon of offense, for stabbing" (*Oxford English Dictionary*). In this sense we can read Peters as Pym's writing instrument, a vehicle for Pym to reach a certain truth about himself. But of course such a penetration (cut, incision, inscription) into the mysteries of Pym's self is fraught with ambiguity from the start, as the writing instrument itself—Dirk Peters—is unfathomable, a blending of whiteness and darkness, of protective friend and ferocious demon. Pym's interpreter (his stylus, as it were) serves only to make more obscure what "truth" is "penetrated"; indeed it is in the very act of penetrating, of desiring such a truth, that the truth is made impenetrable and unattainable.

A more obvious reference to Pym's attempt to penetrate the mysteries of his "journey toward origins" through writing comes with Pym's penknife. Jean Ricardou, who has analyzed some of the metaliterary qualities of *Pym*, claims that when Pym passes his knife blade into the peculiar veined water on the island of Tsalal, he is penetrating something closely resembling a text. Drawing the parallels between a text and the "singular character of the water" (171), Ricardou argues: "If an imaginary perpendicular line is made to sever a given line of writing, the two severed fragments remain united in idea by an intense syntactic cohesion. If, on the other

19. Though we have already described Peters as a maternal figure, the ambiguity of his character also allows him the status of a father figure—perhaps inherited from one of Pym's previous "fathers," *Peterson*.

20. Fiedler, *Love and Death*, p. 396.

21. Pym's dog, Tiger, may also be seen as a kind of interpreter-guide, as he delivers Pym a message from Augustus. But man's best friend is also seen as a potential enemy when Tiger, driven mad by the insufferable conditions of the hold, attacks Pym (82).

hand, a horizontal separation is made between two lines, the broken link, essentially spatial in nature, provides a very inferior sort of adhesion. This double complicity of the liquid with written language—by contiguity and similitude—encourages us to believe that what we are faced with is a text."[22] If this water is indeed a text, it is surely one whose readability is put in question, as we learn that this liquid that flows throughout the island is not at all clear. Says Pym: "Although it flowed with rapidity in all declivities where common water would do so, yet never, except when falling in a cascade, had it the customary appearance of *limpidity*" (171). Though the very next sentence in the narrative affirms just the opposite—that the water is "nevertheless, in point of fact, as perfectly limpid as any limestone water in existence, the difference being only in appearance" (171)— we might do well to heed John Irwin's insight that limpidity or transparency is nothing *but* an appearance and that such a statement must finally be considered ironic or, at the very least, contradictory.[23] Thus suggested is that any sort of writing, any penetration of the blank page (as with a penknife), must render as much obscurity as it does clarity. Inscription here is the very defacement of truth, light, transparency.

In an earlier passage, one that in a certain way parallels the later experience on the island, Pym attempts to penetrate the darkness of his "entombment" in the bottom of the *Grampus*. Having awakened from a state of unconsciousness, Pym searches for a way out—toward lightness, clarity:

I arose, and felt with my fingers for the seams of cracks of the aperture. Having found them, I examined them closely to ascertain if they emitted any light from the stateroom; but none was visible. I then forced the pen blade of my knife through them, until I met with some hard obstacle. Scraping against it, I discovered it to be a solid mass of iron, which, from its pecular wavy feel as I passed the blade along it, I concluded to be a chain cable. (76)

In a way, the "wavy" chain cable repeats itself in the segmented, cable-like stream that Pym confronts on the island of Tsalal; and in this instance, similar implications for writing hold forth. When Pym finally *pen*etrates the dark labyrinthine tunnels of the *Grampus*, he does so to no avail; for his penetration—his "inscription"—does not result in his discovering any light but only another obstacle, and more darkness. We may say, then, that *interpreting* does not get Pym closer to establishing a truth but instead drives him further away, the whole enterprise taking on the aspect of one labyrinth leading into another, with no end in sight. Indeed, the stateroom into which Pym tries to enter, and from which he hopes to gain some light (truth), is nothing less than a labyrinth. Since its most prominent feature is

22. Jean Ricardou, "The Singular Character of the Water," trans. Frank Towne, p. 4.
23. Irwin, *American Hieroglyphics*, p. 155.

"a set of hanging shelves full of books, chiefly books of voyages and travels" (68), we may see the room as a kind of library, in other words, as the site of more references, interpretations, signs.[24] Escape from a textual world is all but impossible for Pym, a fact further confirmed by Pym's journey into what only *seems* to be the world of nature, of purity, of selfsameness—the island of Tsalal.

Contrary to all appearances, Pym's arrival at the island does *not* signal his confrontation with an originary state, with truth, because as we discover, what seems to be a completely natural environment turns out to be no less a "world of lies," of artifice, than Edgarton. As already noted, the water that flows through the island may be said to possess the qualities of a text (according to Ricardou's metaliterary reading); but a perhaps more conclusive indication that writing inhabits this seemingly pure, asymbolic world—a world outside the difference on which writing is based—comes in the peculiar designs of the chasms into which Pym and Dirk Peters venture. Though Pym is never actually convinced there is anything artificial about the chasms,[25] the unnamed author of the final "Note" (207) points out that the chasms, which Pym has sketched in a notepad, are shaped like alphabetical letters: when conjoined with one another they "constitute an Ethiopian verbal root—the root Ꝏ 'To be shady'—whence all the inflections of shadow or darkness" (207). The Note also affirms that the "singular-looking indentures" (195) in the surface of the marl are (despite Pym's conviction to the contrary) works of art. The hieroglyphical appearance is a representation of a human form, and the rest of the indentures are "the Arabic verbal root 'To be white'" and "the full Egyptian word ПꝏꝎPHC, 'The region of the south'" (208). One might say that Pym, while attempting to penetrate into the heart of darkness—into a realm that would represent truth, presence, origins—enters a world literally made of writing, where nature *is* writing. But could it be otherwise, since Pym's writing/representation of the journey is impossible to distinguish from the journey itself?[26]

Of course we need not wholly depend on the text's final voice of authority (in the Note) to realize that a difficulty exists in distinguishing nature from artifice, indeed that the one might be *included* in the other; for even

24. Perhaps the best illustration of the library as denoting an endless deferral of meaning is the story by Jorge Luis Borges, "The Library of Babel," *Labyrinths: Selected Stories and Other Writings*, ed. Donald A. Yates and James E. Irby, pp. 51–58.

25. Pym's "doubt" that the chasm is "altogether the work of nature" (193) is more an expression of amazement at the chasm's features than of true skepticism.

26. It is as if Pym's very interpretation, or representation, of his "journey toward origins" precludes the possibility of his ever encountering those origins, or, as in the words of John Carlos Rowe, "in the very effort of writing such a story that center is displaced, disrupted, deferred" ("Writing and Truth in Poe's *The Narrative of Arthur Gordon Pym*," p. 110). Rowe prefers to see Pym's journey as a movement toward a metaphysical and geographical center.

Pym (who attempts to prove scientifically that the indentures can *only* be the "work of nature") alerts us to the possibility of a confusion between the representation of nature and nature itself. At the site of the first chasm he encounters, for instance, Pym asserts that it is "one of the most singular-looking places imaginable, and we could scarcely bring ourselves to believe it altogether the work of nature" (193); and finding himself near the ruins of a disruptured cliff, he comments that "the surface of the ground in every other direction was strewn with huge tumuli, apparently the wreck of some gigantic structures of art; although, in detail, no semblance of art could be detected" (198). Pym's observation of the landslide that buries thirty-two crew members also invokes the idea that "art" can easily take on the appearance of nature, that one is not always distinguishable from the other. The soapstone hills of Tsalal, he suggests, are stratified in such a way that "every *natural* convulsion would be sure to split the soil into per-pendicular layers of ridges running parallel with one another; and a very moderate exertion of *art* would be sufficient for effecting the same pur-pose" (185, emphasis mine).

That nature and artifice cannot be easily separated, that indeed each may be said to be incorporated in the other, immediately puts in question any conception of the island as a place that is self-identical, or pure. Even the island's most definitive quality, its all-black appearance, turns out to be simply that, an appearance, as we discover that positioned at the very core of this blackness—within the black chasms—are "*white* arrowhead flints" (194, emphasis mine). Moreover, inscribed on the chasm wall, as the Note indicates, is the Arabic verbal root meaning "to be white," further sug-gesting that defilement (or difference) is something completely "natural" to the island. And it should be noted that if the pure black identity of Tsalal is a fiction, we discover also that the pure white identity of that region directly to the south—Tekeli-li—is likewise a fiction. For into the world of "brilliancy and whiteness" (208) comes precisely the sort of "inflections of shadow or darkness" (207) that we find on Tsalal.[27] Indeed, as Pym and Dirk Peters approach the end of their voyage, and sail into the "perfect whiteness" of the sea, we are informed that the "darkness had materially increased" (205). And now standing before them is a collection of images associated with obscurity—curtains, veils, shrouds (all relating to the cata-ract that engulfs Pym).

On his journey, Pym encounters not a world of self-sameness but one of self-difference. Viewing these geographical realms as external manifesta-tions of Pym's psychic journey toward himself, we can now say that the

27. Irwin, *American Hieroglyphics*, p. 204, points out: "And just as whiteness lies at the core of the dark realm of Tsalal, so darkness must be present in the white realm of Tekeli-li, other-wise there could be no color boundary, no figure/ground differentiation, no signification."

culmination of his journey does not signify Pym's return to himself, to a sense of wholeness and unity, but instead points to Pym's "identity" as one that can be understood only in terms of its essential otherness, its *difference*. The "shrouded human figure" that looms before Pym in the final scene is nothing less than a shadowy projection of Pym's own self—his mirror image cast up, and elongated, in the engulfing cataract.[28] In other words, his death (and his life) become precisely his own inscription in "nature."

Though we witness the author's death at the end of the narrative, a final Note—a postscript—attempts to "save" the text, to establish a sense of authority. Here, an unnamed narrator tries to tie up the story's loose ends by suggesting that Pym *did* escape death at sea, only to perish later in an accident of some kind—an accident in which the remaining chapters of the narrative were "irrecoverably lost" (207). He further tells us that Dirk Peters is still alive and could provide an accurate conclusion to Pym's story if he could ever be found. Clearly, authoring the end of *Pym*, bringing the text to a successful closure, is what most interests this unnamed narrator; his very invocation of the problem of the text's open-endedness—and his explanation for the open-endedness—is his way of trying to establish closure. His is a desire to have the final word, to become the text's final authority, and he attempts to satisfy this desire by filling in one of the text's deepest holes—the mystery of the chasm designs.

But in investigating the strange configurations of the chasms, all the author does is lead us back into the text or, rather, into a world made of words, an abyss whose depth turns out to be more language (the writing/ indentures inside the chasm). As Irwin points out, "Thus the note returns the reader to the chasm episode, presumably to retrace the narrative line to the final break in the text, and then on to the note which sends him back to the chasm episode, and so on."[29] But then we realize that even the author of the Note suspects that his "ending" is no ending at all when he remarks: "Conclusions such as these open a wide field for speculation and exciting conjecture. They should be regarded, perhaps, in connexion with some of the most faintly-detailed incidents of the narrative; although in no visible manner is this chain of connexion complete" (208). His reading of *Pym* becomes no more conclusive than Pym's interpretation of his own adventure, and thus it seems that any sort of authority must remain questionable.

---

28. One may easily relate this scene to the previous one in which Pym falls into the embrace of his shadow self, Dirk Peters. Both scenes point to the otherness that is necessary to define oneself.

29. Irwin, *American Hieroglyphics*, p. 196.

The final irony of the Note comes in the text's last line, a quotation: " '*I have graven it within the hills, and my vengeance upon the dust within the rock*' " (208). It is obvious that this sentence, biblical-sounding (though not taken from the Bible), does not belong to the same discourse, the same mode of signification, as do the preceding words; and yet it does set off a problem similar to that embodied in the rest of the Note, as the words attempt to rise to a position of authority with their god-like intonation. If Irwin is correct in saying that the author of these words is not "the Creator of the physical universe, but the creator of the written world of *Pym*,"[30] we should not be surprised to find "within the hills" some clue to the creator's identity. Again, we are directed back into the body of the narrative and are forced to reread the chasms that had apparently just been deciphered. Like other critics, we might see in the strange designs of the chasms (aside from the verbal roots of ancient languages) the creator's initials, "e a p" (𝒜𝒻𝒫), or in the designs of the indentures the author's last name spelled out in reverse, "E O P":[31]

Here, the whole notion of authorship/authority is suddenly made ironic, as the real Poe becomes inscribed in his own narrative—the author graven and in his grave.

30. Ibid, p. 227.
31. For further discussion of how the hills may be read, see Daniel Wells, "Engraved Within the Hills: Further Perspectives on the Ending of *Pym*." Irwin also discusses this problem in *American Hieroglyphics*, p. 228.

II
HAWTHORNE AND MORAL PERSPECTIVISM

Morality is only an interpretation of certain phenomena, more precisely a *misin*-terpretation. . . . [A]s semiotics it remains of incalculable value; it reveals, to the informed man at least, the most precious realities of cultures and inner worlds which did not *know* enough to "understand" themselves. Morality is merely sign-language, merely symptomatology: one must already know *what* it is about to derive profit from it.

—Friedrich Nietzsche, *Twilight of the Idols*

4 THE POISON OF INTERPRETATION
Giovanni's Reading of Rappaccini's Daughter

In the preface to "Rappaccini's Daughter" the narrator who introduces the writings of M. de l'Aubépine/Hawthorne warns the reader that he should "take them [the writings] in precisely the proper point of view" lest they "look excessively like nonsense."[1] But on reading "Rappaccini's Daughter" we begin to wonder if Hawthorne's narrator is not being ironic, since the whole story seems consistently to obscure any "proper" point of view. From the window of his "desolate and ill-furnished apartment" (93), Giovanni Guasconti, a young and impressionable student of science, spies on the story's central scene: the garden where Beatrice Rappaccini tends her beautiful but poisonous flowers. It is from Giovanni's perspective, then, that we understand much of what goes on in the story. But to say that his perspective is the *proper* one—the one that would ultimately make "sense" of the story—is far from adequate; for as we discover, the world that Giovanni observes is not what it appears to be and will not easily yield even to the most scientific investigation. In a sense Hawthorne's story serves as a critique of empirical understanding, but more fundamentally it explores how "truth" is precisely a function of perspective—or interpretation.

We are perhaps already familiar with the way in which *The Scarlet Letter*—published four years after "Rappaccini's Daughter" and anticipated in many respects by the latter story—raises a similar issue of perspectivism. Hester's letter contains only the meaning its observers ascribe to it. When the Puritan community first brands Hester a sinner and makes her stand on the scaffold, we are led to believe that the embroidered letter can only mean "adultery." Later in the novel, after Hester has spent years of her life in penance, performing acts of charity and goodwill, a portion of the community decides to reevaluate the letter's meaning: "many people refused to interpret the scarlet A by its original signification. They said it meant Able; so strong was Hester Prynne, with a woman's strength."[2] But Hawthorne is careful not ever to designate explicitly what the letter means; the word *adultery* is never once mentioned in the course of the narrative—it is only assumed. And *able* becomes simply the opinion of some sympathetic onlookers, affected by Hester's community service. At times Hawthorne even goes so far as to subvert the letter's "original" meaning

---

1. Nathaniel Hawthorne, "Rappaccini's Daughter," *The Centenary Edition*, 10:92. All future references to "Rappaccini's Daughter" pertain to this edition.

2. Nathaniel Hawthorne, *The Scarlet Letter* (hereafter cited in the text as *SL*), *The Centenary Edition*, 1:161.

by adding a perspective that does not at all conform to the predominant one. For instance, during the first scaffold scene, when Hester must encounter "the stings and venomous stabs of public contumely" (*SL*, 57), when she becomes a "spectacle of guilt and shame" (*SL*, 56), Hawthorne suddenly wonders what a Papist might have witnessed had he been among the crowd of condemning Puritans; indeed,

> he might have seen in this beautiful woman, so picturesque in her attire and mien, and with the infant at her bosom, an object to remind him of the image of Divine Maternity, which so many illustrious painters have vied with one another to represent; something which should remind him, indeed, but only in contrast, of that sacred image of sinless motherhood, whose infant was to redeem the world. (*SL*, 56)

Thus Hester, who is as much an emblem of sin as the letter she wears, becomes from another point of view—the Papist's—the very image of saintliness. Does the letter, then, from a different perspective stand for *angel*?

We are as uncertain about what value to attach to the letter as is Hawthorne himself when he first discovers it in the Custom House amid a pile of dusty documents. There is some indication that Hawthorne, through a sympathetic connection with his past, intuits the meaning of the letter, as it burns like "red-hot iron" (*SL*, 32) on his breast. But in the final analysis—which is, as he says, "the analysis of my mind" (*SL*, 31)—Hawthorne does not *discover* the "deep meaning" behind what he refers to as the "mystic symbol" (*SL*, 31) but rather *invents* it by the writing of his narrative. For Hawthorne the letter "gives evidence of a now forgotten art, not to be recovered even by the process of picking out the threads" (*SL*, 31), so what Hawthorne must do in his attempt to unthread the truth of the letter—and of Hester Prynne's life—is *re*thread it in his own fashion, according to his own perspective, and thus create his own *Letter*.

The sort of perspectivist truth implicit in *The Scarlet Letter* (and also, as we shall see, in "Rappaccini's Daughter") may be closely related to the Nietzschean idea of how truth and knowledge are obtained. As one of Nietzsche's modern interpreters, Jean Granier, explains:

> The idea of the fundamental perspectivism of knowledge has as its precise function the uprooting of the metaphysical conviction that subjectivity is capable of dominating the totality of Being. From the start, this notion excludes the possibility that thought can grasp the essence of Being by an immediate intuition [as Hawthorne only *seems* to do when he feels the letter burn on his breast], or that it can constitute a world spread out before the eyes of the spectator-subject. The epistemological subject is necessarily situated, his field of vision is finite; thus, no one perspective can exhaust the richness of reality . . . . By affirming the perspectivism of knowl-

edge, Nietzsche in fact defends an ontological *pluralism:* the essence of Being is to show itself, and to show itself according to an *infinity of viewpoints.*[3]

According to Granier, "The Nietzschean notion of perspectivism overlaps that of interpretation"; and in this regard Granier introduces the example of the historian who shapes and organizes his data "in order to obtain an image of the past that has some rational coherence, and in such a way that the image will never be entirely separable from the personal vision of the particular historian."[4] Similarly in *The Scarlet Letter,* Hawthorne, placing himself in the role of the historian, reinvents Surveyor Pue's outline of the story of the scarlet letter (the document he finds in the Custom House) and thereby turns historic fact into personal vision—the novel. The historic perspective, which supposedly relies only on empirical evidence, cannot help but produce anything more than fiction, the stamp of its own particular viewpoint. As Nietzsche says, "Ultimately, man finds in things nothing but what he himself has imported into them: the finding is called science, the importing—art, religion, love, pride."[5] Such a statement may well be instructive for an understanding of "Rappaccini's Daughter," which, perhaps even more than *The Scarlet Letter,* exemplifies this problem of interpretation.[6] Hawthorne's story not only dramatizes Giovanni's problem of reading the world in a scientific way but also calls attention to our own dilemma as interpreters of the story intent on reaching certain conclusions based on literary "facts."[7]

In reading "Rappaccini's Daughter" we realize that, to a large extent, the problem of Beatrice *is* the problem of the text. Because most of the story's details and events are seen through Giovanni's eyes the reader becomes at once immersed in Giovanni's dilemma of trying to decipher the true nature of one of Hawthorne's most enigmatic heroines.[8] Indeed the reader

3. Jean Granier, "Perspectivism and Interpretation," trans. David B. Allison, in *The New Nietzsche: Contemporary Styles of Interpretation,* ed. David B. Allison, p. 191.

4. Ibid., p. 191.

5. Ibid., p. 195, quotes Nietzsche's *The Will to Power,* no. 606.

6. See Charles Feidelson Jr., *Symbolism and American Literature,* p. 10, who anticipates such discussion by pointing to the epistemological issues implicit in Hawthorne. Regarding *The Scarlet Letter,* Feidelson says: "Every character, in effect, re-enacts the 'Custom House' scene in which Hawthorne himself contemplated the letter, so that the entire 'romance' becomes a kind of exposition of the nature of symbolic perception. Hawthorne's subject is not only the meaning of adultery but also meaning in general; not only *what* the focal symbol means but also *how* it gains significance."

7. The difficulty of truth-finding in any text is summed up by Friedrich Nietzsche in *The Will to Power,* p. 267: "Against positivism, which halts at phenomena—'There are only *facts'*—I would say: No, facts is precisely what there is not, only interpretations."

8. See Roy Male, *Hawthorne's Tragic Vision,* p. 55, who sees Beatrice as "the first of Hawthorne's full developed women—dark, exotic, ambiguous in her 'poisonous' combination of sexual attractiveness and angelic purity. Like Hester Prynne, Zenobia, and Miriam in later books, Beatrice Rappaccini is a prototype of womanhood."

is encouraged to ask, along with Giovanni, what sort of person is Beatrice Rappaccini—human or nonhuman, good or evil, innocent or corrupt, tenderhearted or "poisonous." Gazing down at her from his lofty window, and bewildered by what he sees, Giovanni articulates the problem precisely: "What is this being?—beautiful shall I call her?—or inexpressibly terrible?" (103). Though Giovanni speaks these words almost halfway through the text, it is obvious from the very beginning that his *view* of Beatrice is less than reassuring. As Giovanni only sees Beatrice within the context of her luxuriant garden, he can begin to know her only by the myriad signs that are there set before him; and it is these signs that serve to make confusing, if not contradictory, his—and our—moral evaluation of her.

What Giovanni is first presented with, while looking out of his window, appears to be none other than a Garden of Eden, complete with gushing water, "flowers gorgeously magnificent," and "one shrub in particular . . . that bore a profusion of purple blossoms" (95). For Giovanni, an air of divinity hangs over the garden, as the gurgling sound of water ascends to his window and makes him "feel as if the fountain were an immortal spirit" (94). Divine light even seems to emanate from the gemlike purple blossoms, "so resplendent that it seemed enough to illuminate the garden, even had there been no sunshine" (95). Giovanni perceives a garden not unlike the sort of paradise depicted in Milton's Eden, where

Upon the rapid current, which through veins
Of porous Earth with kindly thirst up-drawn.
Rose a fresh Fountain, and with many a rill
Water'd the Garden. . . .
. . . .
Flow'rs worthy of Paradise which not nice Art
In Beds and curious Knots, but Nature boon
Pour'd forth profuse on Hill and Dale and Plain.[9]

But with the introduction of Dr. Rappaccini into the garden, Giovanni is suddenly given a new set of signs to interpret, signs that would contradict anything resembling a pure and innocent Eden. Rappaccini's mere physical presence—"emacitated, sallow, and sickly-looking" (95)—opposes, and may therefore be considered a corruption of, the fertile environment on which the young man gazes. Moreover, as Rappaccini is seen to avoid going near or inhaling the "vegetable existences," Giovanni comes to recognize the curious scientist as "one walking among malignant influences,

9. John Milton, *Paradise Lost*, in *The Complete Poems and Major Prose of Milton*, ed. Merrit Y. Hughes, book 4, lines 227–30 and 241–43, p. 283.

such as savage beasts, or deadly snakes, or evil spirits" (96). Of course there is already a suggestion of a certain "malignancy" in the garden when, earlier on, we read that some of the plants seem to creep "*serpent-like* along the ground" (95, emphasis mine.) Giovanni, no longer convinced of the garden's sacredness, wonders if what he sees is not a new kind of Eden, only *appearing* to resemble that garden cultivated by the "unfallen parents of the race" (96). He asks himself: "Was this garden, then, the Eden of the present world?—and this man, with such a perception of harm in what his hands caused to grow, was he the Adam?" (96). Giovanni's rhetorical question is really an assertion that what he has stumbled on is only a facsimile of paradise—an Eden constructed by modern science. His mistake is in thinking that Rappaccini is the new Adam when in fact he is the new—and false—God (or man attempting to usurp the power of God with his present-day scientific knowledge).

Following Rappaccini's appearance, Giovanni's attention focuses on Beatrice, who now steps into the garden; and it is she who embodies for him the sort of ambiguous morality with which he has so far been confronted. She is directly compared to the flowers she tends; indeed, when Giovanni sees her it is "as if here were another flower, the human sister of those vegetable ones, as beautiful as they" (97). And though she is identified with nature itself, personifying the kind of purity and innocence we usually associate with the natural, she seems to Giovanni's mind to contain also an element of insidious danger; and in this respect she is no different from the flowers whose "beauty did but conceal a deadlier malice" (96). Natural and innocent, she is somehow also sinister. She is Dante's Beatrice, beautiful and divine, yet she is also the chief inhabitant of what seems to be a fallen world, that of a postlapsarian Garden whose plants are all poisonous.

We should remember that in Hawthorne's world the physical realm is always closely related to the moral one; and any difficulty in perceiving what is put before one's senses often has the result of rendering the world morally ambiguous, if not incomprehensible. Young Goodman Brown, for instance, journeys into the gloom of the forest and consequently sees the dark souls, or sin, of all his supposedly virtuous neighbors and even of his beloved wife, Faith. But we are never quite sure if he himself (as opposed to simply Hawthorne) has allegorized the physical landscape before him and made out of it a moral one, in other words, if his whole experience in the forest is not the product of his overwrought imagination. For as the story suggests, his "evil" experience may have been no more than "a wild dream."[10] No doubt Hawthorne is depicting in this story an essential aspect of the Puritan mind, which sees nature as a text written by God,

10. Nathaniel Hawthorne, "Young Goodman Brown," *The Centenary Edition*, 10:89.

with His signs of morality observable everywhere; but at the same time we must recognize that Hawthorne is also deeply critical—at the very least deeply skeptical—of any solid moral foundation in what appears to be an epistemologically uncertain world.[11] With Giovanni we encounter a perfect example of this problem: the difficulty he has in determining whether Beatrice is good or evil becomes solely dependent on his ability to distinguish reality from fancy, truth from fiction. Indeed, Giovanni's uncertainty as to the exact significance—moral or otherwise—of what he observes in the garden is such that, as the narrator points out, he "could not determine how much of the singularity which he attributed to [Rappaccini and his daughter] was due to their own qualities, and how much to his wonder-working fancy" (98).

As a student of science Giovanni naturally favors an empirical understanding of the world and would like to bring everything he observes in the garden—most especially Beatrice—"within the limits of ordinary experience" (98). And yet as it is strongly suggested, the faculty of the imagination, his "wonder-working fancy," is intensely active and may well be undermining any *factual* interpretation of what he sees. The problem of what Giovanni actually sees and what he only imagines is of course a problem that implicates the reader as well, not simply because Giovanni's point of view appears to be the "proper" one, with which we are meant to identify, but also because the problem must be understood as being intimately connected with Hawthorne's whole aesthetics, that is, with the way in which Hawthorne (or his fiction) *reads* the world. The romance, which is Hawthorne's privileged mode of representation, is described in a well-known passage in "The Custom-House" as occupying that "neutral territory, somewhere between the real world and fairyland, where the Actual and the Imaginary may meet, and each imbue itself with the nature of the other" (*SL*, 36). We may well view the Actual and the Imaginary not only as two separate kinds of reality but also as two distinct modes of representation, neither of which is capable by itself of rendering a truthful interpretation of reality. This is perhaps demonstrated more clearly in the preface to "Rappaccini's Daughter," where the categories of the Actual and the Imaginary become rearticulated in terms of two groups of writers, the Transcendentalists (who represent the Imaginary) and "the great body of pen-and-ink men" (91). It is only *between* these two groups that Hawthorne seems able to occupy a position; for he (Hawthorne/Aubépine) is, "if not too refined, at all events too remote, too shadowy and unsubstantial in his modes of development, to suit the taste of the latter class, and yet too

11. For studies that are largely centered on epistemological problems in Hawthorne, see especially David W. Pancost, "Hawthorne's Epistemology and Ontology," and John T. Irwin, *American Hieroglyphics: The Symbol of the Egyptian Hieroglyphics in the American Renaissance.*

popular to satisfy the spiritual or metaphysical requisitions of the former" (91).

Thus identifying with neither the Transcendentalists nor with the popular (or realistic) writers, Hawthorne finds himself taking the perspective— the interpretive position—of the romancer. Here, though he is at once subject to demonstrating what he calls his "inveterate love of allegory [i.e. the Imaginary]," he is also concerned to instill his writing with "a breath of nature, a rain-drop of pathos and tenderness, or a gleam of humor, [which] will find its way into the midst of his fantastic imagery, and make us feel as if, after all, we were yet within the limits of our native earth [i.e. the Actual]" (91, 92).

For the empirical-minded Giovanni, who desires to comprehend the world only through the physical senses, the world he encounters—which seems to be that "neutral territory . . . where the Actual and the Imaginary may meet"—proves impenetrable. His efforts are spent trying to achieve a "day-light view of Beatrice; thus bringing her rigidly and systematically within the limits of ordinary experience" (105); but try as he does he seems incapable of isolating the realm of the Actual from that of the Imaginary. It should be noted that in Hawthorne "day-light" is usually associated with an actual, undistorted view of the world, whereas seeing during the moonlight hours is equivalent to perceiving the world as though it were imaginary or fantastic (out of the ordinary); and it is precisely these equations that seem to be operating in "Rappaccini's Daughter."[12] But as is often the case in Hawthorne's writing, almost as soon as such equations or associations are made, they are just as quickly undercut by a certain amount of irony. For instance, the narrator at first introduces Giovanni's daylight appraisal of the garden by stating "there is an influence in the light of morning that tends to rectify whatever error of fancy, or even of judgment, we may have incurred during the sun's decline, or among the shadows of the night, or in the less wholesome glow of moonshine" (98). Yet, just when the garden becomes for Giovanni a "real and matter-of-fact" (98) affair, he suddenly decides to see it as a "symbolic language" (98) that would keep him in communion with nature. Indeed, the moment he believes he is witnessing, in the light of day, the garden as it *actually* is, he begins to transform it by allegorizing it, thus turning it into a wholly imaginary landscape, far removed from the "ordinary" sphere.[13]

But Hawthorne's text ironizes the power of empirical understanding in even more apparent ways, for example by suggesting that Giovanni's com-

12. Hawthorne's best articulation of the differences between "daylight" and "moonlight" perception occurs in "The Custom-House" section of *The Scarlet Letter* (SL, 35–36).

13. See Don Parry Norford, who, in "Rappaccini's Garden of Allegory," attempts to equate aspects of the story with Hawthorne's attitude toward art, the garden being "that neutral territory in which allegory flourishes" (p. 173).

parison of Beatrice with a beautiful flower is as much a figment of his imagination as it is an "observation": "Nor did he [Giovanni] fail again to
observe, *or imagine*, an analogy between the beautiful girl and the gor-
geous shrub" (102, emphasis mine). Likewise, when Giovanni spies a
small lizard (or is it a chameleon?) falling victim to the poisonous plants,
the truth of what he sees is suddenly undermined by the narrator's brief
parenthetical remark: "—but, at the distance from which he gazed, he
could scarcely have seen anything so minute—" (102–3).[14] Giovanni is still
testing the powers of his physical senses when, later on, he buys fresh
flowers for Beatrice, to see if they will die on contact with her hands (he
wishes to know if she is indeed poisonous); and indeed, "it seemed to
Giovanni . . . that his beautiful bouquet was already beginning to wither
in her grasp" (104). But again the narrator is careful to remind us that
Giovanni's position, at his lofty window, may not lend itself to truthful
observation, as "there could be no possibility of distinguishing a faded
flower from a fresh one at so great a distance" (104). The validity of Giovanni's "scientific" observations is thus constantly called into question;
and it is no doubt for this reason that Hawthorne's text makes abundant
use of such indefinite expressions as *seemed, as if,* and *appeared,* all of which
serve to make tentative what might otherwise be read as statements of fact.

Of course what Giovanni seeks to discover through his "observations" is
whether Beatrice is poisonous, and therefore whether approaching her
would not somehow endanger his own life. But it should be noted that the
sort of danger Giovanni is threatened by depends largely on the *kind* of
poison he encounters. Like Goodman Brown, Giovanni is inclined to read
into the physical environment certain moral values—and it becomes
obvious from the rhetoric of the text that "poison" comes to signify evil as
much as it does physical contamination. Aside from announcing straight-
forwardly that Giovanni sees Beatrice in terms of "her physical *and* moral
system" (114, emphasis mine) and that for Giovanni "those dreadful pecu-
liarities in her physical nature . . . could not be supposed to exist without
some corresponding monstrosity of soul" (120), the narrator describes the
poison itself in a decidedly moral way. Indeed, what is often referred to as
"vegetable poisons" (100) suddenly takes on a moral connotation when we
read that the "adultery of various vegetable species" appears to Giovanni
to be "no longer of God's making, but the monstrous offspring of man's
depraved fancy, glowing with only an evil mockery of beauty" (110). Fur-

14. At this moment in the story, Giovanni's powers of observation are suggested to be
diminished also by "the wine he quaffed . . . which caused his brain to swim with strange
fantasies in reference to Doctor Rappaccini and the beautiful Beatrice" (101). Drinking, it
should be noted, becomes no less a means for Baglioni to seduce Giovanni to his way of
thinking (in disfavor of Baglioni's rival, Rappaccini) than it is a sign of friendship and goodwill.

thermore, when Giovanni, having been affected by Beatrice, sends forth his own poisonous breath it is said to be "imbued with a venomous feeling out of his heart" (122).

In a penetrating analysis of "Rappaccini's Daughter," Frederick Crews has attempted to see the poison less in moral terms than in terms of Giovanni's sexual fears and desires. He argues:

> If Beatrice's 'poisonousness' accounts for his [Giovanni's] characteristically ambivalent reaction, then that poisonousness may stand for her sexuality as it affects his contrary impulses. Hope and dread wage continual warfare in Giovanni's breast because he fears exactly what he desires. His sexual ambition triggers his fits of revulsion, for the closer he comes to Beatrice, the more he is appalled by her implied sexual power.[15]

Crews cites several passages in the text that are rife with sexual connotation; for example, when Beatrice approaches the shrub, we read that she "threw open her arms, as with a passionate ardor, and drew its branches into an intimate embrace; so intimate, that her features were hidden in its leafy bosom, and her glistening ringlets all intermingled with the flowers" (102). Here Giovanni, who is watching Beatrice, "fearfully imagines himself in the place of the erotically smothered branches." Furthermore, in arguing for the connection between the poison and sexuality, Crews points out that "whenever Giovanni makes semi-intentional amatory advances, what literally checks him is a fear of poison."[16] Thus Crews cites the passage where Giovanni yearns to touch Beatrice and thus remove the physical barrier that stands between them:

> On the few occasions when Giovanni had seemed tempted to overstep the limit, Beatrice grew so sad, so stern, and withal wore such a look of desolate separation, shuddering at itself, that not a spoken word was requisite to repel him. At such times, he was startled at the horrible suspicions [suspicions apparently of her poisonousness] that rose, monster-like, out of the caverns of his heart. (116)

Crews's point that the story is best read as a psychological allegory of Giovanni's sexual anxieties does not, however, warrant a dismissal of moral or religious readings, such as that provided by Roy Male's earlier study of the story.[17] For in no way should we consider the moral issues implicit in "Rappaccini's Daughter" as irrelevant to the story's psychosexual concerns, especially given the kind of Christian (or perhaps we should say, Puritan) perspective to which Giovanni seems to subscribe.

15. Frederick Crews, *The Sins of the Fathers: Hawthorne's Psychological Themes*, p. 119.
16. Ibid., pp. 122, 121.
17. Male, *Hawthorne's Tragic Vision*, pp. 54–70.

According to Nina Baym, it is typical of the Puritan ideology, in which Hawthorne's writings are so immersed, to view as immoral "anything which is self-expressive" (such as one's sexuality or natural instincts); indeed, Baym says, "Human nature is represented as evil in order that man be persuaded to submit to control and confinement."[18] We may say that Giovanni adopts this sort of Puritan mentality, as he tries to control human nature—indeed nature itself—by imposing on Beatrice's sexuality a certain moral value, that is, evil. In the sense that Giovanni sees Beatrice as being secluded from society, showing as she does "such lack of familiarity with modes and forms, that Giovanni responded [to her questions] as if to a child" (112–13), she becomes for him the very emblem of nature. It is only when Beatrice demonstrates her natural passions—which is to say, that part of her that reveals itself as untamed, energetic, and excessive[19]—that he begins to find her morally corrupt (poisonous). For Giovanni, the realm of the garden that Beatrice inhabits lies outside the moral-rational system with which he attempts to comprehend the world; and for this reason he sees it at times as "fierce, passionate, and even *unnatural*" (110, emphasis mine). Indeed, for Giovanni, it is ungovernable nature that is unnatural, and it is the artificial world of conventions that is natural.[20]

The kind of immorality ascribed to nature is the same kind we see attributed to Pearl in *The Scarlet Letter.* Having lived with her mother mainly outside the established community, Pearl is utterly oblivious to social convention and so behaves like a wild child, sometimes substituting (like Beatrice) the natural world for human society. We read, at one moment in the narrative, that the "great black forest" becomes "the play-mate of the lonely infant" (*SL*, 204). Yet as she is a child who often takes on the qualities of "that wild, heathen Nature of the forest" (*SL*, 203)—possessing as she does a "fierce temper" (*SL*, 94) and easily capable of bursting into fits of passion—Pearl's unruliness is viewed by the community (and by her own mother for that matter) as something "outlandish" and "unearthly" (*SL*, 94) and, therefore, "a shadowy reflection of . . . evil" (*SL*, 94). Calling her witch-like or elfish thus becomes a way for the Puritan mind to secure as well as to define itself against a disorderly—and amoral—Nature.

For Giovanni, gaining mastery over nature means comprehending it

18. Nina Baym, "The Romantic *Malgré Lui:* Hawthorne in the Custom House," p. 21.

19. I refer to *excessive* in the sense that Beatrice, like the flowers she resembles, cannot be contained within normal bounds; she overflows with passion, as she is said to look "redundant with life, health, and energy" (97).

20. See Kent Bales, "Sexual Exploitation and the Fall from Natural Virtue in Rappaccini's Garden," p. 139, whose "moral" reading of the story points out, "To accept Giovanni's judgment as normative, then, is to accept the conventional and ordinary as 'natural' and to reject the unconventional, fierce, and passionate as 'unnatural.'"

fully. But the irony of his attempt to *know* nature is that the moment he imposes on it a system of knowledge, be it scientific or moral, he can no longer be said to possess a truthful understanding of nature; he can no longer recognize nature behind the artificial system he has laid over it. It is suggested, for instance, in the very beginning of the story that Giovanni has brought to his understanding of Beatrice (and hence of the nature she represents) a Christian system of belief; for as the narrator is careful to point out, Giovanni is "not unstudied in the great poem of his country [meaning Dante's *Divine Comedy*]" (93), in which "Beatrice" plays an important role. Because of his reading of Dante, Giovanni is predisposed to see Beatrice as the Italian poet depicted her—as a pure and divine woman. But though this is so, it becomes apparent that Giovanni is equally inclined to see Beatrice from a much darker perspective. As it is reported that he may well be occupying the same mansion as once did a person whom Dante pictured as "a partaker of the immortal agonies of the Inferno" (93), the physical "scene" Giovanni inhabits suddenly takes on the aspect of a moral position. His outlook on the world is now influenced by visions of hell; and no doubt his opinion that the Paduan sunshine is less bright and cheerful than that of his own southern Italy indicates the darker moral light in which he will "see" Beatrice.

It should be noted that in Hawthorne a true understanding or knowledge of the other is obtained only by one's possessing a certain *sympathy,* a concept, according to Roy Male, that Hawthorne inherited from the German and English romanticists. Male notes that for the romantics, including the American Transcendentalists, "Sympathy emphasized man's link with man and with nature; served as a sort of intuitive and image-making 'sixth' sense which was glorified above unimaginative sagacity."[21] The notion of sympathy plays a significant role in Hawthorne's epistemology, its primary characteristic here being, as David Pancost points out, "the mind's imaginative identification with the object of its contemplation—for a moment, the mind becomes a work of art or another person."[22] Through sympathy the truth is revealed, as when Hawthorne, in the Custom House, places the scarlet letter over his heart and is suggested to intuit its "deep meaning," feeling it "subtly communicating itself to my sensibilities, but evading the analysis of my mind" (*SL,* 31). It is the "heart" that serves as Hawthorne's most powerful symbol for conveying the concept of sympathy, and thus we often find that the only relatable truth seems to be that of the human heart. At times Hawthorne even measures his worth as a writer of romances (for instance, in the preface to *The House*

21. Roy Male, "Hawthorne and the Concept of Sympathy," p. 149.
22. Pancost, "Hawthorne's Epistemology," p. 11.

of the Seven Gables) by how well he manages to convey the truth of his *own* heart, and so form a sympathetic relationship with his readers.[23]

But though it is important to understand what "sympathy" means for Hawthorne, as well as how he invokes it in his writings, it is perhaps more important to realize that Hawthorne is highly skeptical of this romantic idea as a real possibility. Hardly having the "deeply-grounded belief in organicism" that Male contends he has,[24] Hawthorne seems all too aware of postlapsarian man's inability to communicate and understand in a natural, or sympathetic, way. As Edgar Dryden points out, for Hawthorne the natural man (and the "Gentle Reader") no longer exist; gone is that "world of sympathetic involvement, . . . where understanding imposed no burden and an innocent interpretation was possible." Quoting from Hawthorne's *The Marble Faun*, Dryden argues that it is language itself that is mainly responsible for Hawthornian man's alienation from himself and from nature:

"Before the sophistication of the human intellect formed what we now call language," the world interpreted itself "without the aid of words." In the place of language that seeks through endless analogies to mediate the distance now existing between man and nature, there once was a power of sympathy that brought all parts of existence together and allowed them to communicate instantly and completely.[25]

In "Rappaccini's Daughter" we are at times given to believe that Giovanni *does* enjoy moments of sympathetic understanding and thus obtains a full, unmediated comprehension of the object of his contemplation, that is, of Beatrice. But on careful examination of Hawthorne's text, we see that such moments are invariably made ironic. When Giovanni, for instance, enters Beatrice's garden, which is referred to as "the *heart* of the barren city" (98, emphasis mine), one may interpret this to mean that Giovanni has finally "connected" with Beatrice in a sympathetic way; yet we must remember that his movement into the garden is merely a physical penetration, and seen in epistemological terms, it becomes a manifestation of his desire to know the world through the physical senses—empirically.[26] Of course, since a sympathetic understanding is strictly an intuitive or spir-

23. Nathaniel Hawthorne, *The House of the Seven Gables*, in *The Complete Works of Nathaniel Hawthorne*, 3:13, writes in the preface that the "Romance," as a work of art, "sins unpardonably so far as it may swerve aside from the truth of the human heart." In "The Custom-House" section of *The Scarlet Letter*, Hawthorne shows great concern for the author's ability to "stand in some true relation with his audience" (*SL*, 4).
24. Male, "Concept of Sympathy," p. 149.
25. Edgar A. Dryden, *Nathaniel Hawthorne: The Poetics of Enchantment*, p. 128. The Hawthorne quotations refer to *The Centenary Edition*, 4:249, 258.
26. Crews, *Sins of the Fathers*, p. 123, sees Giovanni's penetration into the garden in plainly sexual terms, the description of it being "virtually pornographic."

itual process, it cannot be obtained empirically; yet even so, we are further assured that no "connection" is made between Giovanni and Beatrice when, as already pointed out, the two lovers fail even to make physical contact. The irony of this "penetration" into the "heart" of the barren city is perhaps emphasized even more by the intimation that the chambermaid, Lisabetta, despite her apparent religiosity (she is constantly mouthing Christian oaths) has few spiritual intentions in escorting Giovanni to the private entrance of Beatrice's garden. Indeed, when Giovanni gives her the gold that, as she claims, "Many a young man in Padua would give . . . to be admitted among those flowers" (108), it is as if to suggest she is leading him into a brothel.

More explicit examples of what appears to be Giovanni's "sympathetic understanding" are found in the text, and these often relate to his seeing Beatrice in a pure light, her true self finally presenting itself to the young student-observer. At times Giovanni seems to shun any kind of empirical understanding of Beatrice, convinced that "there is something truer and more real, than what we can see with the eyes, and touch with the finger" (120). This is another version of Beatrice's dictum: "If true to the outward senses, still it may be false in its essence" (112). Relinquishing any strong commitment to empirical thinking, he thus seems able to appreciate Beatrice in a wholly *natural* way; and at moments he is said to relate to her innocently, "like a brother" (113) or like a playmate (115). A definite sympathetic connection between them is indicated when the narrator says "they had looked love, with eyes that conveyed the holy secret from the depths of one soul into the depths of the other" and "they had even spoke love, in those gushes of passion when their spirits darted forth in articulated breath, like tongues of long-hidden flame" (115–16). (In terms of the latter quotation, one may recall Arthur Dimmesdale's ideal of communicating sympathetically to his congregation by speaking with a "Tongue of Flame" [*SL*, 142].) This sort of sympathetic understanding may well be related to Emerson's belief that man, once he is steeped in the spirit of nature, becomes "a transparent eyeball," capable of perceiving the world purely and immediately. As Emerson wrote in his essay *Nature:*

In the woods, we return to reason and faith. There I feel that nothing can befall me in life,—no disgrace, no calamity (leaving me my eyes), which nature cannot repair. Standing on the bare ground,—my head bathed in the blithe air, and uplifted into infinite space,—all mean egotism vanishes. I become a transparent eyeball; I am nothing; I see all; the currents of the Universal Being circulate through me; I am part or particle of God. . . . In the tranquil landscape, and especially in the distant line of the horizon, man beholds somewhat as beautiful as his own nature.[27]

27. Ralph Waldo Emerson, *Nature,* in *The Collected Works of Ralph Waldo Emerson,* 1:10.

We may well assume that Hawthorne's text is referring precisely to such Transcendentalist notions when Giovanni appears to "gaze through the beautiful girl's eyes into her transparent soul" (112) and when it is elsewhere said that "the pure fountain [of Beatrice's heart] had been unsealed from its depths, and made visible in its transparency to his mental eye" (122).

But whatever sympathetic knowledge of Beatrice that Giovanni is suggested to have is quickly made ironic by the fact that he still *sees* superficially, that is, he lacks any kind of spiritual insight. Though he is said to witness the "pure light of her [Beatrice's] character," it is made clear that his seeing her this way is owing more to "her high attributes, than . . . any deep and gracious faith, on his part" (120). In other words, Giovanni cannot seem to resist viewing the world according to empirical "evidence" (120) and hence cannot resist submitting the world (nature, Beatrice) to "some decisive test that should satisfy him" (120). It is hinted that he is possessed of a certain egotism (or lack of sympathy) that prevents his being able to know the world, or any person, in a profound way. The "vanity to be expected in a beautiful young man" apparently prompts Giovanni "to look at his figure in the mirror," a gesture that, as the narrator says, becomes "the token of a certain shallowness of feeling and insincerity of character" (121). As he cannot see and feel deeply, he tries to find a richness of value in his own physical features, not ever considering what lies below those surface details: "He did gaze, however, and said to himself, that his features had never before possessed so rich a grace, nor his eyes such vivacity, nor his cheeks so warm a hue of superabundant life" (121).

Giovanni's lack of sympathy is further suggested by the many references to his defective heart. We are told, for instance, at the very outset that as an impressionable young man he has "a tendency to heart-break" (93); later, Baglioni mockingly refers to the possibility of Giovanni's having some kind of "disease of body or heart, [since] he is so inquisitive about physicians" (99); and then Giovanni himself wonders, after becoming increasingly obsessed with the beautiful and tempting Beatrice, "if his heart were in any real danger" (105). We can interpret Giovanni's "heart problem" in a number of ways—as emotional, physical, and/or moral in nature—but still there is no escaping the overriding *spiritual* (or sympathetic) implications of the "heart," to which the narrator refers explicitly when he remarks: "Guasconti had not a deep heart . . . but he had a quick fancy" (105). Later, the narrator suggests something similar about Giovanni's heart when he intimates that the young student does not really express true love, only "that cunning semblance of love which flourishes in the imagination, but strikes no depth of root into the heart" (115). Giovanni's heart having no depth, he thus becomes incapable of seeing the world sympathetically or truthfully—the only "truth" he sees is that which he imagines.

At those moments when Beatrice seems to reveal herself to him, when her true self becomes present, we discover that Giovanni is actually reading this "presence" into her, covering her over or distorting her with his *re*-presentation of her, his invention of her. The instant that he believes he finally sees her, that her being comes to light, is described thus:

> She was human: her nature was endowed with all gentle and feminine qualities; she was worthiest to be worshipped; she was capable, surely, on her part, of the height and heroism of love. (114)

The irony of this passage is that Giovanni, thinking he sees Beatrice in all her simplicity—no longer a monstrous being capable of poisoning him but rather an ordinary human being—immediately glorifies her and so transforms her into a heroic character, someone belonging to the realm of fiction. This sort of glorification of Beatrice is rearticulated in another passage, when Giovanni comes before Beatrice's "actual presence" in the garden. Here he believes he sees her as she *really* is:

> . . . with her actual presence, there came influences which had too real an existence to be at once shaken off; recollections of the delicate and benign power of her feminine nature, which had so often enveloped him in a religious calm . . . recollections which, had Giovanni known how to estimate them, would have assured him that all this ugly mystery was but an earthly illusion, and that, whatever mist of evil might seem to have gathered over her, the real Beatrice was a heavenly angel. Incapable as he was of such high faith, still her presence had not utterly lost its magic. (122)

Again Giovanni is seen to fall under the illusion that he gains a truthful understanding of Beatrice when in fact what he sees is his own invention of her as "a heavenly angel." Her presence is no presence at all but, as the narrator points out, is "magic": it is a fiction that Giovanni beholds. The additional irony of the passage reveals itself in the fact that Beatrice's "true self" comes to light only in Giovanni's *recollection* of her, not in her "actual presence." Earlier, we notice that Giovanni warns Baglioni, "The recollection of a perfume—the bare idea of it—may easily be mistaken for a present reality" (117–18), a statement that alerts us to the idea that memory—anyone's—cannot be trusted to render a truthful representation of reality. Instead, what recollection does is impose a past reality on what is considered to be a "present reality," thus falsifying and making impossible the existence of that latter reality. In recalling Beatrice to mind, Giovanni does not succeed in obtaining a more truthful interpretation of her but rather ends up undermining her "presence"—indeed he *absents* her through his re-creation of her.

In a way Giovanni becomes as much of an artist-figure (a creator) in the story as Dr. Rappaccini, who constructs the *art*-ificial garden and is even once specifically referred to as an "artist" (126). The position of the artist in Hawthorne is, as it turns out, not far removed from that of the empirical scientist, who falls into the same dilemma as any interpreter, no matter how "factual" he believes his interpretation to be. Instead of revealing a truth about the world, interpretation *creates* that truth, a process by which the interpreter, whether he be an artist or a scientist, is always remaking the world according to his own perspective.[28] This means, of course, that such modes of representation as we have already discussed—the actual and the imaginary—become indistinguishable from each other, the factual being impossible to separate from the fictive. Even Baglioni, who prides himself on his "ordinary" view of reality, must resort to "art" to validate his own particular sort of truth. He does this mainly by discrediting his archrival in the world of science, Rappaccini, suggesting through his "story-telling" that Rappaccini's science is "poisonous" (defective, harmful, false). Though Baglioni does relate an actual story that influences Giovanni—an "old fable of the Indian woman" (118) who, because of her poisonousness, had once threatened the life of Alexander the Great—it is also his very language, his words, that attempt to seduce Giovanni into distrusting the validity of Rappaccini's science, his "truth." It is as if each time he speaks to Giovanni about Rappaccini's supposed evil (usually by calling attention to Beatrice's "poisonousness"), he leaves "what he had said to produce its effect on the young man's mind" (119). Thus it is not surprising that Giovanni is so affected by "a light or injurious *word*" (118, emphasis mine) from Baglioni, as rhetoric itself seems to be the power behind the latter's "truth."[29]

We may say that it is precisely language, or interpretation, that subverts the natural world that Beatrice and her garden apparently represent. Early on in the story we are already alerted to the fact that Beatrice's "innocent"

28. Granier, "Perspectivism and Interpretation," p. 193, points out that "The interpreting subject is not like the conscientious philologist who labors over deciphering a manuscript; he throws himself into interpretation with the same energy that fires his appetite for living, for growth, for conquest. The *act* of interpreting is the surge of life. . . . [W]hat we call the original 'text' . . . must contain a kind of fundamental *indetermination* that leaves open a free field for the individual's *creative* activity."

29. The end of the story gives Baglioni the final word, and indeed we see him standing above, in a God-like position, at the window where Giovanni once stood. Though he appears triumphant, the scientific "truth" that he possesses is made ironic by the fact that his antidote to the poison serves instead to kill Beatrice—which is the result of *his* experiment (128).

world is corrupted by the "sin of art,"[30] as we see her garden being related to artwork, "so happily arranged that it might have served a sculptor for a study" (95). Beatrice herself is described in terms of art, seeming as she does to be always emerging "from under a sculptured portal" (97), as if she were a figure in the sculpture suddenly coming to life. But it is not until Giovanni "poisons" the garden with his own interpretations, his own words, that Beatrice's corruption is dramatized to its fullest extent. Finally being convinced of her evil, of her "poisonousness," Giovanni no longer has to agonize over what he should call her, name her: "Beautiful . . . or inexpressibly terrible." His words "Accursed one!"—which he cries "with venomous scorn and anger" (124)—allow us to believe that he has at last come around to forming an unqualified opinion about Beatrice; he has decided on a "truth" for her.

But as we see, it is precisely the poisonous person he declares her to be that he himself becomes with his outcry, or rather it is the words themselves, which he uses to define and dominate her (and by extension, nature itself), that become the real poison—the venom—of the story. Indeed the emphasis of Giovanni's "sin" against Beatrice is placed on his "terrible words" (124). As the narrator remarks, no earthly happiness could be possible "after such deep love had been so bitterly wronged as was Beatrice's love by Giovanni's blighting words" (126). More than simply offending her delicate sensibilities, Giovanni's words appear to contaminate her very being. As she says, "Oh, what is death, after such words as thine?" (125). And her final statement thus serves to link the poison of his own "nature" with that of the interpretive power of language: "Thy *words* of hatred are like lead within my heart—but they, too, will fall away as I ascend. Oh, was there not, from the first, more poison in thy nature than in mine?" (127). Her last comment is suggestive, for it points to the fact that Giovanni's mere *viewing* of her is "from the first" never an innocent act but is always an act of interpretation or investigation, which would preclude any leap of faith, or blind belief, on his part.

Though Giovanni, Baglioni, and Rappaccini all share responsibility for "poisoning" Beatrice's garden with their interpretive languages (the two elder scientists acting as mediating father figures in respect to Giovanni's "own" way of perceiving Beatrice)[31], not one of these characters by himself

30. The "sin of art" is an expression I borrow from Crews, p. 158, who asserts that in Hawthorne "art and guilt are intertwined." Ethan Brand, for example, is a kind of artist figure who, in searching for the Unpardonable Sin, ends up committing it. In Hawthorne, interpreting (or allegorizing) itself becomes a sin, as it precludes faith. For a discussion of how Hawthorne criticizes the act of allegorizing, see John O. Rees, Jr., "Hawthorne's Concept of Allegory: A Reconsideration." I am, however, using the word *sin* here only in the sense of a stain on, or a distortion of, the natural.

31. Baglioni is constantly identifying himself as an old friend of Giovanni's father, in other words, as a kind of substitute father who wants to protect Giovanni from the world's evil.

can be said to hold a primary or proper perspective on Beatrice, if for no other reason than that the "symbolic language" (as Giovanni thinks of it) that is imposed on, and corrupts, all that lies inside the garden imposes itself *outside* the garden as well. Indeed, what John Franzosa has called "the language of inflation" exceeds the confines of the garden and finds its way into almost every aspect of Hawthorne's story, thus reducing the possibility of anyone's having authority over the "reality" in which he is steeped.[32] What seems to be outside the garden is really part of the garden, the flowers of rhetoric (let us call them) extending themselves into what only appears to Giovanni to be the "barren" world of the city. As Franzosa says, "The language of inflation is present in the very extravagance of the writing," and thus he concludes, "Like Giovanni, the reader receives a superabundance of images that challenges his capacity to regulate and systematize."[33] With its allusive and "symbolic" language, the text has the effect of tempting the reader—almost in the same way that Beatrice and her garden "tempt" Giovanni—to read allegorically, in effect to become exactly the type of empirical scientist, or interpreter, that is characterized in the story (subject to the same errors of interpretation).

This lack of an authoritative or proper point of view makes itself apparent even in the story's preface, which "heads" the text and is supposed to articulate the author's truth, his Word. If there is ever to be a proper point of view, it should be the author's; but here—as in the subsequent narrative—the problem of distinguishing between fact and fancy is once again played out, leaving any notion of a central truth in question. The narrator of the preface begins with "fact," telling us: "We do not remember to have seen any translated specimens of the productions of M. de l'Aubépine; a fact the less to be wondered at" (91). But of course what proposes itself to be a factual introduction to the story becomes just another demonstration of the "imaginary" blending with, becoming indistinguishable from, the "actual." Aubépine, as it turns out, is only an imaginary re-creation of Hawthorne, as all of the stories with which Aubépine is credited were actually written by Hawthorne (but with their titles translated into French).[34] In attributing the original authorship of the story to Aubépine (a

---

Rappaccini, suggested to be planning to wed the young student to his daughter, also becomes a father figure (a potential father-in-law) to Giovanni. Both "fathers" manipulate Giovanni, "poison" his mind with their empirical and imaginative perspectives; in effect, they school Giovanni in their own poisonous art of interpretation.

32. John Franzosa, "The Language of Inflation in 'Rappaccini's Daughter.'"

33. Ibid., p. 7.

34. In the preface, pp. 92–93, Aubépine ("Hawthorne") is said to have been the *original* writer of the collection of stories entitled "*Contes deux fois racontées*" (*Twice-Told Tales*) and of such other stories as "*Le Voyage Céleste à Chemin de Fer*" ("The Celestial Railroad"), "*Le nouveau Père Adam et la nouvelle Mère Eve*" ("The New Adam and Eve"), "*L'Artiste du Beau; ou*

fictional self), Hawthorne thus places himself in the position of translator of his "own" work, which makes the text of "Rappaccini's Daughter" but another of his many "twice-told" tales. All of this dramatizes the idea that authorship or proper ownership of a text is a kind of fiction, that the "author" is really only a translator of some prior text which no doubt is itself a translation. Indeed, what the author becomes here is a displaced figure, displaced by the reader who with each new reading reinvents, reauthors, the work before him. In the role of reader, Hawthorne thus can be said to hold no more authority, no more proper a point of view, than does his "own" character Giovanni.

Unlike his Puritan ancestors and the Transcendentalists of his own time, Hawthorne realized that language cannot overcome its own "poisonous" influences and that, far from being an innocent activity, interpretation (his own writing, for example) cannot help but reflect one's own selfish desire to gain mastery over the world. It seems that all "readers" in Hawthorne— whether they be Giovanni, Goodman Brown, Coverdale, Reverend Hooper, or Hawthorne himself—serve only to poison the world with their various interpretations; indeed they can do nothing else but cast on an otherwise "pure" world some sort of belief system, or moral evaluation, that would pollute both themselves and whatever natural and innocent realm they might conceivably yearn for. The problem here may point to Hawthorne's concern not only about the kind of "sin" that reading engenders but also about the political implications of such reading/writing, that is, about the power of a certain doctrine or system of belief to hold sway over an entire community of people, whether that community resides in Salem or in Brook Farm. Keenly aware of the manipulative power of language, Hawthorne thus attempts to undermine authority or the idea of some "final word" (what could only be God's and not man's) by allowing us to see the irony implicit in any authoritative gesture.

---

le Papillon Mécanique" ("The Artist of the Beautiful"), and "Béatrice; ou la Belle Empoisonneuse" ("Rappaccini's Daughter").

III
MELVILLE AND THE FICTION OF SOCIAL JUSTICE

The "purpose of the law" . . . is absolutely the last thing to employ in the history of the origin of law. . . . [T]he cause of the origin of a thing and its eventual utility, its actual employment and place in a system of purposes, lie worlds apart; whatever exists, having somehow come into being, is again and again reinterpreted to new ends, taken over, transformed, and redirected by some power superior to it; all events in the organic world are a subduing, a *becoming master,* and all subduing and becoming master involves a fresh interpretation, an adaptation through which any previous "meaning" and "purpose" are necessarily obscured or even obliterated.

   —Friedrich Nietzsche, *On the Genealogy of Morals*

5 THE VIOLENT FORMS OF TRUTH IN
BILLY BUDD, SAILOR (AN INSIDE NARRATIVE)

The curious "sequel" that comes at the end of *Billy Budd, Sailor (An Inside Narrative)* poses for us, perhaps most obviously, the question of the Handsome Sailor's true character.[1] What exactly is it? We are given to believe throughout Melville's short novel that Billy Budd is the very emblem of innocence, an Adam before the Fall; yet the last two "sequels" (chapters 29 and 30) seem to be devoted exclusively to distorting that image, with portrayals of Billy that vary significantly from the view to which we are most predisposed by the main narrative. Of course the representations that are given here are not supposed to be the narrator's own. The one in chapter 29, describing Billy as a vindictive murderer and ringleader of a mutiny plot, is an obvious falsification of the facts reported in a naval chronicle under the title "News from the Mediterranean" (130). The other, in chapter 30, is a ballad written by another foretopman, entitled "Billy in the Darbies." This is a kind of commemorative poem that, though it seems at first glance to idealize the young sailor, actually renders a Billy Budd who is neither simple nor innocent, one who indulges in double meanings and wordplays (suggested in the lines, "O, 'tis me, not the sentence they'll suspend / Ay, ay, all is up; and I must up too" [132]) and one who has probably had intimate associations with unwholesome port women (suggested in the line, "Like the eardrop I gave to Bristol Molly" [132]).[2] But even though the narrator does not claim responsibility for these apparent misrepresentations of Billy's character, we are left wondering why they should constitute the greater part of a sequel whose initial purpose is to demonstrate the "truth uncompromisingly told" (128).

We can perhaps easily justify these brief "portraits" by arguing that the narrator is simply setting them off in ironic contrast to his own portrait of the Handsome Sailor, trying to convince us that *his* manner of representing Billy is the more accurate one. In this way the narrator would be able to attain a sense of authority that cannot be attributed to other, less adept interpreters of the Billy Budd affair, interpreters who, unlike himself, cannot boast of having had an "inside" view of the events. But then the question arises as to how the narrator can possibly separate his "inside story" from the sequel that is still contained within it. Are not these supposedly

---

1. Herman Melville, *Billy Budd, Sailor (An Inside Narrative)*, ed. Harrison Hayford and Merton M. Sealts, Jr., p. 128. All future references to *Billy Budd* pertain to this edition.
2. The ironies of the poem "Billy in the Darbies" have been previously pointed out by Paul Brodtkorb, Jr., "The Definitive *Billy Budd*: 'But Aren't it all Sham?'" p. 607, and by Edgar A. Dryden, *Melville's Thematics of Form*, pp. 214–15.

distorted views of the Handsome Sailor—the naval report and the poem—
also a part of the overall portrait that is *Billy Budd*? If so, then how are we to
determine which is the proper narrative (or the narrative proper) and
thus, by extension, the proper reading of the hero Billy Budd?[3] How do we
know what is the "real" story?

To a large extent, Melville's last novel does not allow any more of an
understanding of Billy's true character than his earlier work *Moby-Dick*
allows of the White Whale. What "truth" about Billy Budd we do obtain
seems to depend solely on whatever representation is imposed on him
(similar to the way Moby Dick *becomes* the various discourses—scientific,
historic, religious, literary—that make up Ishmael's narrative). In contrast
to most critics who would like to see Billy as the incarnation of pure innocence—and Claggart as the incarnation of pure evil—we should recognize
that in *Billy Budd* Melville reveals no more fondness for comprehending
the world in allegorical terms than he does in *Moby-Dick*, where Ishmael
may well serve as Melville's spokesman when he refers disparagingly to
those landsmen-interpreters who "might scout at Moby Dick as a monstrous fable, or still worse and more detestable, a hideous and intolerable
allegory."[4] It is precisely allegory's pretense to make a direct correlation
between "ideas" and "things" that Melville's texts constantly seek to
undermine, as Charles Feidelson has astutely pointed out, and in this matter *Billy Budd* is no exception.[5] Indeed, though we are tempted at every
step to read the novel as an allegorical tale of the conflict between good and
evil, what we discover instead is something more on the level of a Nietzschean "genealogy of morals," that is, an investigation and critique of the
origin and development of any such moral system. Similar in spirit to
Nietzsche's project, Melville's novel becomes less interested in telling the
truth (moral or otherwise) of a certain story than in telling the story of
"truth" itself. In particular, it dramatizes how all truth becomes merely a
product of those forces that have, by a will to power, come into positions of
authority.[6] Whether those forces come to be represented by Captain Vere,

3. Though a number of critics have argued that Vere is the true hero of the tale—the most
important figure in *Billy Budd*—my contention that Billy is the hero rests on the narrator's own
reference to Billy as "the main figure" (53) in his story. See H. Bruce Franklin, "From Empire
to Empire: *Billy Budd, Sailor*," in *Herman Melville: Reassessments*, ed. A. Robert Lee, p. 202,
whose moral analysis argues similarly. My concern is not so much with Melville's overall
intentions as with what the narrator offers as *his* intentions.

4. Herman Melville, *Moby-Dick*, p. 177.

5. See Charles Feidelson, Jr., *Symbolism and American Literature*, especially pp. 28–35. For
analyses that view *Billy Budd* as a major departure in Melville's thinking, one that represents
the author's final reconciliation with the world, see E. L. Grant Watson, "Melville's Testament
of Acceptance," and Nina Baym, "Melville's Quarrel with Fiction."

6. See Friedrich Nietzsche, *On the Genealogy of Morals*, trans. Walter Kaufmann, pp. 25–26,
who writes that "the source of the concept 'good' has been sought and established in the
wrong place: the judgment 'good' did *not* originate with those to whom 'goodness' was

by Claggart, or by the narrator himself, *Billy Budd* finally makes clear that the "forms" (128) of truth that make possible man's operation in the world—that give him a sense of moral and metaphysical stability—are maintained only through the same surges of violence and disorder they purport to regulate and control.

From the beginning of *Billy Budd*, when the narrator first compares Billy to the type known as the "Handsome Sailor" (43), we are prepared to understand the young seaman-hero on the most allegorical level—as the embodiment of innocence and virtue. Possessing a "natural regality" (43), Billy is indirectly associated with the noble savage from Africa who is uncorrupted by civilization, an association that becomes more explicit when the narrator later refers to Billy as "a sort of upright barbarian, much such perhaps as Adam presumably might have been ere the urbane Serpent wriggled himself into his company" (52). Indeed, this "child-man" (86) seems to have less connection with normal society than he does with "unadulterate Nature" (120), with the dogs, horses, and songbirds to which he is regularly compared. He is

one to whom not yet has been proferred the questionable apple of knowledge. He was illiterate; he could not read, but he could sing, and like the illiterate nightingale was sometimes the composer of his own song. (52)

Blonde-haired and blue-eyed, Billy Budd resembles a typically angelic character, his physical beauty an outward manifestation of his moral nature; so inexperienced is he with "the diabolical incarnate . . . in some men" that he appears to carry about him a "serene and happy light" (119), one no doubt expressive of his absolute purity of soul. It is not surprising, therefore, that in the final chapters of his life Billy is depicted as something of a Christ figure, his hanging scene—his "ascension" at the yardarm—becoming an obvious reference to the New Testament accounts of Christ's Resurrection.

Yet though the narrator of the story seems inclined to maintain this romantic vision of Billy Budd (as if he had decided on a neatly allegorical structure for his narrative), we should understand that there exist certain ambiguities about the narrator himself, ambiguities that would call into

---

shown! Rather it was 'the good' themselves, that is to say, the noble, powerful, high-stationed and high-minded, who felt and established themselves and their actions as good, that is, of the first rank, in contradistinction to all the low, low-minded, common and plebian. It was out of this *pathos of distance* that they first seized the right to create values and to coin names for values. . . . [T]he protracted and domineering fundamental total feeling on the part of a higher ruling order in relation to a lower order, to a 'below'—that is the origin of the antithesis 'good' and 'bad.' "

question the very truthfulness of his report, of what he claims as his "inside narrative."[7] First of all, what exactly does he mean by *inside*? If the word implies that the narrator has some firsthand knowledge of the Billy Budd affair, are we to assume that he was on board the *Bellipotent* during Billy's impressment and subsequent execution there? And if so, just how close was he to the "secret facts of the tragedy" (131)?

From the little information we are given about the narrator's identity—an identity that finally remains unclear—we may suppose that, were he on board the ship, he most likely served in the capacity of a naval officer. Given his extremely eloquent style of speech (which employs numerous literary references), he could hardly have been a common sailor like Billy Budd. If he resembles anyone on board the *Bellipotent*, it is most definitely the bookish Captain Vere, who is said to have "a marked leaning toward everything intellectual" (62). Moreover, it seems, through the various statements he makes, that the narrator sympathizes with the naval officer's point of view: he characterizes the Nore Mutiny, for example, as an incident that involved "transmuting the flag of founded law and freedom defined, into the enemy's red meteor of unbridled and unbounded revolt" (54); and later he alludes to the "unswerving loyalty of the marine corps" (55) as having been directly responsible for putting down the violent insurrection of an "aggressively insolent" (55) crew. But still, any such notion of the narrator's identity must be considered sheer speculation. For all we know he may never have served in the British navy or even been to sea; he may have been no more than a politically conservative landsman, as some critics contend.[8] Of course, his being a landsman—and hence an outsider to the whole affair—would immediately make suspect the authenticity of his "inside" narrative and would thus suggest that he is but another of

7. See Lawrance Thompson, *Melville's Quarrel with God*, p. 360, whose ironic reading of the novel revolves mainly around the idea that "Melville arranges to let us see that the narrator is...just a wee bit stupid." I would argue, however, that Melville's text, more cunning than Thompson figured, also holds up the possibility that the narrator (not exactly ignorant) is really something of a deceiver, a confidence man. The distinction between total innocence (ignorance) and total deception is not an easy one to discern in Melville, as my reading intends to demonstrate. For a penetrating analysis of the narrator's unreliability, and of the consequential questioning of Billy's "essential innocence," see Lyon Evans, Jr., " 'Too Good to be True': Subverting Christian Hope in *Billy Budd*." I am much indebted to Evans's essay for pointing out many of the ambiguities in Billy's and Claggart's moral characters. Whereas Evans's essay serves humanistic ends, mine attempts to see a more radical indeterminacy at work: the "real" Billy, the "real" Claggart, are nowhere to be found but in the *act* of representing. Evans ends up remystifying Billy in terms of the historic empiricism practiced by the so-called Higher Critics of the New Testament (empiricism of any kind, as I argue, is for Melville just one of the many "forms" that violate—or do violence to—the truth).

8. See Evans, " 'Too Good to be True,' " p. 328, who sees the narrator as identifying with an officer's perspective. I argue, however, that the narrator may be no less inscrutable than Billy Budd; and his point of view—as I later argue—is impossible to discover because it consists of points of view *other* than his own.

Melville's famous confidence men, apt to display more finesse than frankness.[9]

There is some evidence in the text to indicate that even if the narrator had been on board the ship, he did not have firsthand knowledge—or an "inside view"—of the events. The most obvious example of this occurs during Vere's closeted interview with Billy, after the latter has already been "formally convicted and sentenced to be hung" (114). Here the narrator confesses, "Beyond the communication of the sentence, what took place at this interview was never known"; and thus all he can offer in the way of enlightenment are "some conjectures" based on what he believes to be Billy's and Vere's character (114). We should note that even prior to this final interview with Billy, *only* the three main characters of the novel are said to be present at the scene of Claggart's death (another "closeted" scene); thus the narrator's knowledge could be only secondhand. There are other scenes too that would seem to preclude the narrator's presence, such as when the afterguardsman, under the cover of night, approaches Billy and seemingly tries to enlist the young sailor into the service of an unnamed conspiracy. The secrecy that surrounds this episode gives one to believe that the narrator most probably received his account of it by way of rumor.

But perhaps we need only notice the narrator's rather tentative (or evasive) language to realize his lack of familiarity with the many occurrences on board the *Bellipotent*. For instance, at one moment he writes, "What he [Claggart] said...was to the effect following, if not altogether in these words" (92); and when Billy, before his execution, is denied communication with anyone but the chaplain, the narrator comments that "certain unobtrusive measures were taken absolutely to insure this point" (118). That the narrator fails to define those "measures" may well suggest that he does not know what they were, a likely possibility for someone not possessing an "inside view."

If the narrator's report of the Billy Budd affair demonstrates itself to be unreliable, how then are we to estimate the character of the Handsome Sailor, around whom the entire "inside" story revolves? Indeed, we might begin to see certain ironic undercurrents that run throughout the narrator's depiction of Billy Budd, undercurrents that would serve to contradict the idea of Billy as a model of moral perfection and, perhaps even beyond that, to show him as someone capable of sharing those same "evil" qualities that belong to his supposed allegorical opposite, John Claggart. As early as the second chapter, the narrator's irony about the truth of Billy's character begins to assert itself, with mention of the "mysteriousness" (51)

9. In his attempt to idealize the common sailor, the narrator remarks, in chapter 16, "The sailor is frankness, the landsman is finesse" (86).

that seems to pervade the sailor's very being. Here we discover that instead of having a fixed and recognizable identity, Billy Budd is suddenly represented as a figure whose outward expression tends to elude definition. Trying to explain the peculiar responses that Billy's presence elicits from his fellow shipmates, the narrator points out:

> . . . he [Billy] showed in face that humane look of reposeful good nature which the Greek sculptor in some instances gave to his heroic strong man, Hercules. But this again was subtly modified by another and pervasive quality. The ear, small and shapely, the arch of the foot, the curve in mouth and nostril, even the indurated hand dyed to the orange-tawny of the toucan's bill, a hand telling alike of the halyards and tar bucket; but, above all, something in the mobile expression, and every chance attitude and movement, something suggestive of a mother eminently favored by Love and the Graces; all this strangely indicated a lineage in direct contradiction to his lot. (51)

The sheer contradictoriness of Billy's physical appearance (which exhibits both masculine and feminine qualities), together with what is suggestively called his "mobile expression," serves to indicate that Billy Budd cannot be made to conform to a stable type, let alone be fully comprehended—hence his "mysteriousness."

We are further alerted to Billy's mysterious character when the narrator attempts to locate the *source* of his mystery in the sailor's origins. By offering the "facts" of Billy's historic beginnings, the narrator thus hopes to make the mysteriousness somehow "less mysterious" (51), as he says. He proceeds to recount a verbal exchange between Billy and the receiving officer on board the *Bellipotent*, an exchange that addresses the problem of Billy's heritage.

> Asked by the officer, a small, brisk little gentleman as it chanced, among other questions, his place of birth, he [Billy] replied, "Please, sir, I don't know."
> "Don't know where you were born? Who was your father?
> "God knows, sir."
> Struck by the straightforward simplicity of these replies, the officer next asked, "Do you know anything about your beginning?"
> "No, sir. But I have heard that I was found in a pretty silk-lined basket hanging one morning from the knocker of a good man's door in Bristol." (51)

Though the narrator is quick to assume from the last statement that Billy is evidently of "noble descent" (52), it should not, however, escape us that the story of the "silk-lined basket" and of Billy's being left at a "good man's door" is only a rumor that Billy hears, not at all what the narrator earlier contends is a "matter of fact" (51). The real fact of the matter is that Billy's beginnings are, as the sailor's words tell us, unknown. By presenting this dialogue between Billy and the *Bellipotent* officer, the narrator in no way elucidates the sort of mystery that surrounds Billy's character; instead he succeeds only in obscuring that character even further with the introduction of *another* mystery.

For the narrator of *Billy Budd*, Billy's mysteriousness does not in the least present a problem for interpretation but, on the contrary, is all the more proof that the young sailor is a noble man, both socially and morally.[10] But the irony of the narrative reveals itself in the fact that the story's most villainous character—the master-at-arms, Claggart—is described in almost exactly the same "mysterious" terms. The narrator writes of him that "he looked like a man of high quality, social and moral, who for reasons of his own was keeping incog. Nothing was known of his former life" (64–65). Like Billy Budd, Claggart appears to have about him an air of nobility, yet (again like Billy) all we ever learn about his previous life ashore comes by way of "rumor"—there is a "dearth of exact knowledge as to his true antecedents" (65). That the text should implicitly draw such striking parallels between these two seemingly contrasting figures leads one to suspect that Billy Budd's mysteriousness, like Claggart's, may indicate something "shady" or "dark" about his moral character.

Our only glimpse of Billy Budd prior to his impressment on the *Bellipotent* is when he is serving on the English merchantman the *Rights-of-Man*, under the command of Captain Graveling; and it is here that Billy is supposed to have experienced a relatively simple and innocent life among a "happy family" (47) of sailors. In this "former and simpler sphere," as the narrator calls it, Billy seems to have dwelled in an atmosphere that was almost Edenic, far removed from the "ampler and more knowing world of a great warship" (50).[11] In fact, it was Billy himself—as Graveling attests—who instilled this happy atmosphere aboard the *Rights*, which was formerly a "rat-pit of quarrels" (46). But Billy's moral behavior immediately comes under suspicion the moment we consider just *how* this sort of untroubled, near utopic environment was created.

Hearing Graveling's account of Billy's influence on the other seamen, one is led to believe that Billy's mere presence—with the "virtue [that] went out of him" (47]—was all that was needed to turn an otherwise quarrelsome crew into a family of peace-loving sailors. This is to suggest that the men on the *Rights* learned to be virtuous simply by following Billy's

10. For the narrator, as well as for many critics, Billy's mysteriousness is automatically associated with holiness. H. Bruce Franklin, *The Wake of the Gods: Melville's Mythology,* p. 189, for example, sees Billy Budd much in the same way as he sees Bartleby: both appear to be mysterious and meek and therefore divine or Christ-like. Franklin apparently sees no difference between the narrator's representation of Billy and Melville's own intentions.

11. Many critics interpret Billy's transfer from the *Rights-of-Man* to the *Bellipotent* in an allegorical way, marking Billy's movement from paradise to the world of sin. See, for example, Harold Beaver's introduction to *Billy Budd, Sailor and Other Stories,* pp. 41, 46–47.

example. But perhaps a more likely possibility is that Billy, with his inordinate physical strength, inspired among his fellow seamen more fear than he did love and kindness. In the example of his beating up of the troublemaker Red Whiskers, who is said to have taunted Billy "out of envy," Billy is supposed to have transformed this bully into a peaceful and loving creature; yet who can honestly believe that after having endured "half a minute" of a "terrible drubbing," Red Whiskers "now really loves Billy" (47)?[12] One may detect Melville's irony behind Graveling's observation that when Billy came on board the *Rights*, "it was like a Catholic priest striking peace in an Irish shindy" (47); the word *striking* here, besides having the meaning of impressing deeply, also carries the connotation of violent action, the type of action in which Billy is not afraid to engage. Also, when Graveling uses the phrase "virtue went out of him," we are reminded of a similar-sounding phrase used to describe the moment when Billy kills Claggart: "his right arm shot out" (99). Indeed, on board the *Rights-of-Man* it seems that Billy Budd was as much of a fear-inspiring law enforcer as is Claggart on the *Bellipotent*; and because of his ability to maintain order with the use of his fists, the title with which we most often associate Claggart—"master-at-arms"—can perhaps be more appropriately applied to Billy.[13]

One might argue, of course, that Billy's display of his physical prowess—that is, his being a "fighting-peacemaker" (48)—does not in any way indicate malicious or "evil" intentions on his part but rather is completely in keeping with the narrator's romantic conception of sailors in general. The narrator says that "as a class, sailors are in character a juvenile race. Even their deviations are marked by juvenility" (87). Just what these "deviations" are, we are never told; that they may be connected to the way in which sailors sometimes act in a violent manner is suggested in an earlier passage, where the narrator points out that "less often than landsmen do their [sailors'] vices, so called, partake of crookedness of heart, seeming less to proceed from viciousness than exuberance of vitality after long constraint: frank manifestations in accordance with natural law" (52). Thus, as the narrator describes it, any violation (or act of violence) in which sailors such as Billy Budd might engage is strictly of an innocent sort—instinctual rather than premeditated.

But, we may ask, just how much credence can we give to such an idealized view of sailors, especially in light of the way Melville often portrays sailors (as a class) in his fiction? In the man-of-war world of *White-Jacket*,

12. See Evans, " 'Too Good to be True,' " p. 342.
13. That Graveling's account of Billy is not to be trusted may be hinted in the fact that Graveling possesses the same deceptive qualities as the "naturally depraved" Claggart: he is "respectable" and he has a musical voice (45).

for instance, we witness sailors who are typically given to fighting, thievery, and debauchery. Indeed, the narrator of this early novel states: "What too many seamen are when ashore is very well known; but what some of them become when completely cut off from shore indulgences can hardly be imagined by landsmen. The sins for which the cities of the plain were overthrown still linger in some of these wooden-walled Gomorrahs of the deep."[14] We discover that even the narrator of *Billy Budd* (perhaps in a moment of blindness) contradicts his own romantic point of view by calling attention to some of the seamier aspects of the common sailor. While speculating on Claggart's shadowy past he points to the fact that, because of the urgency of "keeping up the muster rolls" (65) during politically turbulent times, many of those who were drafted into the British navy were of the lowest class, sometimes "culled direct from jails." The narrator also mentions, "Insolvent debtors of minor grade, together with the promiscuous lame ducks of morality, found in the navy a convenient and secure refuge" (65). Depicted in this manner, sailors could hardly be characterized as a "juvenile race"; the suggestion is that their "deviations" aboard ship would tend to be less innocent than criminal in kind.

No doubt one reason it becomes difficult to believe there could be anything immoral about this most handsome of sailors, Billy Budd, is that the narrator often insists on having us see a correspondence between Billy's splendid physical appearance and his inner moral nature. He reports early in the novel:

The moral nature was seldom out of keeping with the physical make. Indeed, except as toned by the former, the comeliness and power, always attractive in masculine conjunction, hardly could have drawn the sort of honest homage the Handsome Sailor in some examples received from his less gifted associates. (44)

But we should perhaps recognize from Melville's other sea novels that being a Handsome Sailor does not necessarily imply that one is pure and innocent. In *Redburn*, for instance, we encounter another handsome sailor, Harry Bolton, who takes the young Redburn to London to visit one of "the lowest and most squalid haunts of sailor iniquity," a male brothel.[15] Though it cannot be said that Billy is ever clearly defined as a homosexual—he is too mysterious to be precisely defined in any way—the important point to be made is that his "beauty," supposedly representing his inner goodness, often becomes connected with a certain sexual power he exerts over his fellow seamen. The ambiguous smiles (51) with which Billy

14. Herman Melville, *White-Jacket, or The World in a Man-of-War*, in *The Writings of Herman Melville*, 5:375–76.
15. Herman Melville, *Redburn*, in *The Writings of Herman Melville*, 4:234.

is greeted when he first comes on board the *Bellipotent* could hardly be called "honest homage." Indeed, possessing "feminine" (50) features similar to those attributed to Harry Bolton, Billy seems to incite the prurient interest of everyone from the old Dansker (who slyly studies his "Baby Budd" with "a certain grim internal merriment" [70]) to Captain Vere (whose sudden attraction to Billy leads him to contemplate how "in the nude [Billy] might have posed for a statue of Adam before the Fall" [94]). Even Claggart, Billy's archantagonist, finds himself strangely drawn to the Handsome Sailor, so much so that he "could even have loved Billy but for fate and ban" (88). It is in the soup-spilling incident, as critics have aptly noted, that the homoerotic implications of Billy and Claggart's relationship become most apparent: here we are told, in sexually suggestive terms, that the "greasy liquid" Billy sends "streaming" before Claggart's feet provokes in the master-at-arms a "profound passion" (78).[16]

At one moment in the text the narrator is willing to admit that the Handsome Sailor does indeed have a flaw, that "like the beautiful woman in one of Hawthorne's minor tales, there was just one thing amiss in him," this being "an occasional liability to a vocal defect" (53). Yet, despite this admission, it becomes obvious with such phrases as "just one thing amiss" and "occasional liability" that the narrator is trying to minimize the importance of this flaw, to show that it is inconsequential. And, even though the narrator is intent on attributing Billy's "imperfection" (53) to the work of that "arch interferer, the envious marplot of Eden [i.e., Satan]" (53), still we are never given to believe that Billy himself is capable of engaging in any sinful activity. In fact, we can even say that depicting Billy with a vocal defect may be a kind of ploy on the narrator's part to reaffirm the Handsome Sailor's romantic status, to see him once again as a total innocent—a Caspar Hauser figure, inarticulate, preverbal.[17] We realize that it is Billy's frustrated attempt to speak that is indirectly responsible for his killing Claggart, but the narrator makes us acutely aware that Billy's action is in no way a sign of iniquity—rather it comes in "accordance with the frank manifestations of natural law." Thus, in terms of the way the narrator would like us to perceive Billy, this solitary flaw—this "organic hesitancy" (53)—turns out to be wholly consistent with the Handsome Sailor's identification with "unadulterate Nature."

But as we have seen, what the narrator seems to intend does not always harmonize with what his narrative reveals (as though the narrator is somehow blind to the implications of what he himself is saying, or as though the

16. The sexual content of this passage has been previously noted by, among others, F. O. Matthiessen, *American Renaissance: Art and Expression in the Age of Emerson and Whitman*, p. 506.

17. See Franklin, *Wake of the Gods*, for a detailed discussion of Billy as the inarticulate innocent (refer to note 10).

narrator, playing the role of confidence man, purposely deceives). For although we may sometimes be prompted to see Billy as a kind of preverbal innocent, Melville's highly ironical text also allows us to view the young sailor as someone quite capable of manipulating language for his own purposes, even to the point of lying. We notice that following his nocturnal meeting with the suspicious afterguardsman, Billy feels compelled to report the incident to the old Dansker; yet what he finally gives to the Dansker is not the true story but "only a partial and anonymous account" (85). Before the drumhead court, Billy does not even offer a "version" (85) of what happened; instead, when asked if "he knew of or suspected aught savoring of incipient trouble . . . going on in any section of the ship's company" (106), he simply refuses to say anything about his earlier experience with the afterguardsman and so responds in the negative. In each of these incidents the narrator attempts to excuse Billy's odd behavior by suggesting that the well-intentioned sailor does not wish to involve himself in the "dirty work of a telltale" (85). But no matter how the narrator tries to preserve Billy Budd's "essential innocence" (121), the fact remains that Billy has consciously distorted the truth—an action *not* characteristic of Adam before the Fall.

There are a few other indications throughout the novel that Billy is no stranger to the world of artifice and duplicity (products of a fallen world), and these include references to his "spinning yarns" (68) while in the foretop and engaging in "sportful talk" (72) with his messmates.[18] At the trial scene, Billy declares in his defense, "I have eaten the King's bread and I am true to the King" (106), and thus betrays a marked facility for using figurative language, something we do not expect from one supposedly given over to "straightforward simplicity" (51). The narrator, not surprisingly, tries on various occasions to reassure us that Billy's words are of a purely innocent kind, that there is indeed (even despite Billy's occasional stuttering) a certain naturalness about Billy's language that manifests itself in a "singularly musical" voice (53), one that is capable of delivering syllables "in the clear melody of a singing bird" (123). But here the idea of associating a sweet-sounding, musical voice with innocence is at once put in question by the fact that the "evil" master-at-arms, John Claggart, is also said to possess a musical voice, one that, like the siren's song, is employed primarily for deceptive purposes. When the Dansker warns Billy that Claggart has a "sweet voice" (71), he means to imply that the master-at-arms' words of affection for Billy are not to be trusted; and when Claggart, dur-

18. These references serve to reveal that Billy is capable of a certain playfulness in his speech that is not associated with "pure" or "natural" language. Here we are made to think that the portrait of Billy in the poem "Billy in the Darbies"—where he is shown as one who can play with words and create double meanings—is more accurate a representation than we had once supposed.

ing the soup-spilling scene, comments in a "low musical voice . . . ,
'Handsomely done, my lad! And handsome is as handsome did it, too!' "
(72), it is clear that his words are intended not only to mock the Handsome
Sailor but to mislead him as well. By suggesting (through Claggart) that a
certain musicality in one's voice may well be a sign of duplicity, Melville's
narrative thus allows us to consider the possibility that Billy Budd is
merely *playing the part* of the Handsome Sailor, acting the innocent.[19] But,
of course, we are prevented from finally ever knowing whether Billy is
being deceptive or not, as "something more, or rather something else than
mere shrewdness is perhaps needful for the due understanding of such a
character as Billy Budd's" (90).

If the allegorical structure of *Billy Budd* begins to break down with the
evidence gathered "against" Billy's innocence, we might do well to see
how the other side of the story—Claggart's evil—is likewise called into
question. The narrator would have us believe that there is something fundamentally corrupt at Claggart's moral core, and he suggests as much
when he first introduces the master-at-arms in obviously negative terms,
comparing him, in certain of his physical features, first to the infamous
Indian chief Tecumseh[20] and then to the Reverend Titus Oates, who in the
time of Charles II was "the fraud of the alleged Popish Plot" (64). Claggart,
moreover, is described as having a pallid complexion that seems to hint of
"something defective or abnormal in the constitution and blood"; this,
combined with the fact that his brow is "of the sort phrenologically associated with more than average intellect" (64), prepares us to understand the
master-at-arms as an archetypal villain, closely resembling *The Scarlet Letter*'s Roger Chillingworth.[21] But are we perhaps rushing to conclusions if
we assume, as the narrator does, that Claggart's outward appearance
implies that he is "the direct reverse of a saint" (74)? Could it be, rather, that
Claggart's appearance of evil is no more than that, an appearance?
    By carefully examining what is said about Claggart, we realize that our
(and the narrator's) perception of him as a villainous character is based for

19. Billy's role-playing ability is suggested in a statement that the narrator makes: "But an
innate repugnance to playing a part at all approaching that of an informer against one's own
shipmates . . . prevailed with him" (106-7). Though Billy chooses not to play this dastardly
part, we are still given to believe that he does go on to "play" another "part" instead.
    20. Although we can suppose that the narrator is trying to associate Tecumseh with some
sort of evil, we should be aware that other, more modern historians have portrayed the Indian
chief in a more sympathetic light. See Samuel Eliot Morison, Henry Steele Commager, and
William E. Leuchtenburg, *The Growth of the American Republic*, 1:363–65, who view Tecumseh
not as the stereotypical savage on the warpath but rather as "a lithe, handsome, and stately
warrior," trying to "counteract an American policy which threatened to wipe out [his] people; as eventually it did."
    21. For a comparison between Claggart and Roger Chillingworth, see the editorial notes by
Harrison Hayford and Merton Sealts, Jr., in *Billy Budd, Sailor*, p. 172.

the most part on unreliable information. It is mainly through the testimony of "certain grizzled sea gossips" that we learn that Claggart, during his previous life ashore, may have been involved in a "swindle" for which he was eventually brought to trial. But such testimony becomes at once questionable the moment the narrator makes clear that "nobody could substantiate this report" (65). Indeed, all we ever discover about Claggart's history seems to come by way of rumors spread by those men aboard ship who would be most apt to malign the master-at-arms. As the narrator remarks: "But the less credence was to be given to the gun-deck talk touching Claggart, seeing that no man holding his office in a man-of-war can ever hope to be popular with the crew." And even if they did not bear malice toward Claggart, the crewmen would be likely to distort the truth about him in any case, since "sailors are much like landsmen: they are apt to exaggerate or romance it" (66–67).

The narrator tries to show a "vague plausibility" (65) in the sailors' gossip about Claggart by presenting historic evidence that criminals did indeed often find their way into the ranks of the British navy, especially during such politically volatile periods as that in which the story is set. He tells us, for instance, that it was a common occurrence for warships short of hands to fill their deficient quotas by enlisting men "direct from the jails" (66). But this piece of information is made to seem not all that reliable, as the narrator claims to have obtained it from a "book I cannot recall." Perhaps as a way to reassure us about the authenticity of the report, he proceeds to mention that "the same thing was personally communicated to me now more than forty years ago by . . . a Baltimore Negro, a Trafalgar man" (66). But here again we encounter a problem, as we wonder if the distance in time (forty years) has not in some way distorted the memory of what was originally said to the narrator. Moreover, since the information was related by a Trafalgar man, we may also wonder if the latter did not "exaggerate or romance it," as sailors are known to do.

One of the main reasons we come to suspect Claggart of villainy is the repeated suggestion that he is covertly operating to destroy Billy Budd, that he is indeed the chief orchestrator of those "strange experiences . . . on board the *Bellipotent*" (86) that seem specifically designed to discredit the Handsome Sailor, that is, the sabotaging of Billy's gear and the afterguardsman's attempt to bribe Billy. But if we closely examine the various references made to these incidents, we discover that there is no way to prove conclusively that the so-called "strange experiences" are traceable to Claggart. Indeed, so undetermined is Claggart's involvement in these incidents that it becomes impossible to say with certainty whether the master-at-arms is "secretly down on" (73) Billy in the first place.

It is the old Dansker who first intimates that Claggart is plotting against Billy when, supposedly offering his "wise counsel" (69) concerning Billy's messed-up gear, the Dansker tells Billy that "Jemmy Legs (meaning the master-at-arms) is down on you" (71). But just how reliable is the opinion of this old grizzled sea gossip? As already pointed out, such veteran sailors are not usually to be trusted, especially when their talk revolves around as unpopular a figure aboard ship as the master-at-arms. From a man like the Dansker, who is said to have been "subordinated lifelong to the will of superiors" (71), we can expect little more than a negatively biased account of Claggart.

That the Dansker's accusation against Claggart may be completely fanciful is given further credence after the soup-spilling incident, when a sailor named Donald shows surprise at such a view as that expressed by the Dansker. Here, apparently flattered by Claggart's reference to his being a Handsome Sailor, Billy exclaims: "There now, who says that Jemmy Legs is down on me!" (72–73). To which Donald replies with a certain amount of surprise, "And who said he was, Beauty?" Donald's remark, which seems to be made in all sincerity, thus prompts Billy to feel foolish, "recalling that it was only one person, Board-Her-in-the-Smoke [the Dansker], who had suggested what to him was the smoky idea that this master-at-arms was in any peculiar way hostile to him" (72–73). At this moment in the narrative, Donald's point of view seems to Billy—and perhaps to the reader as well—to have more validity than that of the eccentric old Dansker.

And finally, we should recognize that the incident regarding Billy's gear, instead of having the ominous import that the Dansker seems to think it has, may be, as Lyon Evans has pointed out, nothing more than a sailor's malicious prank. After hearing about Billy's misfortune, one of the topmates responds cynically, "Is it your bag, Billy? . . . Well, sew yourself up in it, bully boy, and then you'll be sure to know if anybody meddles with it" (69). The topmate's play on Billy's name ("bully boy") may well suggest that Billy's reputation for beating up Red Whiskers on the *Rights-of-Man* has followed him onto the *Bellipotent*, possibly provoking some of Billy's current shipmates.[22]

The Dansker is also the one who is primarily responsible for suggesting both to Billy and to the reader that Claggart is at the bottom of the afterguardsman's attempt to bribe the Handsome Sailor (a bribe whose purpose would be to implicate Billy in a mutiny plot). Again, in his characteristically cryptic manner, the Dansker responds to Billy's deep concern over the incident by saying, "*Jemmy Legs* is *down* on you." Learning from Billy that it was someone else—not Claggart—who was directly involved in the bribery attempt, he goes on to exclaim, "Ho, it was an afterguardsman, then. A cat's-paw, a cat's-paw!" (85). As the narrator tells us, "cat's-paw" either may be a reference to the afterguardsman—as an

22. See Evans, "'Too Good to be True,'" p. 337.

agent for Claggart—or it may simply refer to "a light puff of air" that the Dansker suddenly notices "coming over the calm sea" (85).[23] It is the para-tactical structure of the Dansker's latter statements (a structure that, in omitting connectives or transitional phrases, makes ambiguous the causal relationship between one sentence and another) that creates such "obscu-rity" that the narrator is forced to admit "there is no telling" (85) which of the word's meanings the Dansker has in mind. Thus the Dansker only helps to confuse the issue of whether the afterguardsman is truly a repre-sentative of Claggart's supposed ill will.

If the Dansker's words make it difficult to determine the meaning of Billy's nocturnal meeting with the afterguardsman, so also do the few elliptical remarks of the afterguardsman during the scene in question. When "the stranger" approaches Billy in a retired nook of the ship, he is said to whisper: "We are not the only impressed ones, Billy. There's a gang of us.—Couldn't you—help—at a pinch?" (82). Uncomprehending, Billy asks the strange man, "What do you mean?" In reply, the man holds before Billy's eyes two glittering objects, presumably guineas with which to bribe Billy, saying "see, they are yours, Billy, if you'll only—"; at this point Billy, with "resentful eagerness" (82), interrupts the man with a threat to toss him over the taffrail if he does not return to his proper place on the ship.

Our tendency here is to assume that the afterguardsman is tempting Billy to join with a gang of impressed sailors who are "plotting disaffec-tion" (90) aboard ship; but because of the studied ambiguity of Melville's text we do not once hear a direct reference to a mutiny plot, and thus we can do no more than speculate that this is what the afterguardsman is actually intending. That the man's request may be more innocent than Billy imagines is perhaps indicated by his being "confounded" (82), or sur-prised, by Billy's sharp reaction to the request he never finishes making.[24] Indeed, when Billy spies the man on the following afternoon, the latter appears to be "the last man in the world . . . to be overburdened with thoughts, especially those perilous thoughts that must needs belong to a conspirator in any serious project, or even to the underling of such a con-spirator." His "familiar sort of friendly recognition" of Billy, as well as his enthusiastic show of "good-fellowship" a day or two later, seems to bespeak the man's innocence and thus to mock Billy's conviction that the attempted bribe "must involve evil of some sort" (84).[25]

23. See Harold Beaver's notes in his edition of *Billy Budd*, p. 462, where a "cat's-paw" is explained as "not only 'a light puff of air' but, more equivocally, 'a person used as a tool,' especially, among sailors, 'a seaman used to entice volunteers.' "
24. This observation has been made also by Terence J. Matheson, "A New Look at Clag-gart," p. 446.
25. The irony of Billy's interpretation of the afterguardsman's action reveals itself most acutely in the fact that Billy, supposedly knowing nothing of evil, would therefore not be able

Another possibility that we must consider is that Claggart, never wishing to frame Billy, actually believes the Handsome Sailor is involved in some conspiracy to overtake the ship. It may be that Squeak, one of Claggart's "more cunning corporals" (79), is responsible for making Billy appear to the master-at-arms as a "dangerous man" (94). Since we know that Squeak frequently "pervert[ed] to his chief certain innocent frolics of the good-natured foretopman [i.e., Billy]" (79), he may have given Claggart a corrupted version of what really took place during Billy's meeting with the afterguardsman and thus may have made the entire episode seem part of an evil plot in which Billy was clearly involved.[26] Because we are told that Claggart "never suspected the veracity of [Squeak's] reports" (79) we may conjecture that Claggart, when accusing Billy of plotting to mutiny, is simply acting with good intentions on the information he obtains from his supposedly "faithful understrapper" (79). Claggart, then, would have to be seen not as a malicious liar intent on bringing Billy down but rather as a patriotic officer who is trying as best he can to preserve law and order among the ship's company.[27]

One final possibility remains that would seem to clear Claggart of the charge that he is maliciously framing Billy (and consequently that he is, as the narrator claims, a perfect example of "Natural Depravity" [75]).[28] Perhaps Billy *is* guilty of conspiring with other sailors. As evidence for this, we can point to a fact that we have already mentioned in connection with Billy's possible corruption: Billy's lying to the drumhead court about possessing any knowledge of "incipient trouble" aboard ship. That Billy would deny having secretly met with the afterguardsman and having been witness to apparently rebellious talk is enough to bring some suspicion on the Handsome Sailor. Furthermore, when Billy cannot answer the court's question as to why Claggart (who accuses Billy of mutinous activity) should have "so maliciously lied," we might imagine—as would "some observers"—that Billy's state of confusion here is really a betrayal of his

---

to identify it.

26. We may also consider the possibility that Squeak may have himself set the traps for Billy, not only planning the bribe (or even actually doing the bribing, since Billy is not really sure whom he sees in the dark), but also sabotoging Billy's gear.

27. See Evans, " 'Too Good to be True,' " p. 339.

28. The very way in which "natural depravity" is characterized by the narrator should make us wary of the term as a credible description of Claggart's essential nature. As the narrator tells us, those individuals who are naturally depraved are almost impossible to detect, so consistently do they fold themselves within "the mantle of respectability" (75). Indeed, such is their talent for purposeful disguise that the most predominant aspect of their personality—their irrationality—is "to the average mind not distinguishable from sanity" (76). The question therefore arises, if this is a true account of the naturally depraved person, how then can the narrator, with *his* average mind, detect the insanity beneath Claggart's sane appearance? For an analysis of other ironies in the narrator's description of "natural depravity," see Brodtkorb, "The Definitive *Billy Budd*," p. 604.

"hidden guilt" (107). Though the narrator tries to convince us that it is merely Billy's innocence that is to blame for his present tongue-tie, we cannot help but wonder if, as in the previous instance, it is a case of Billy's *reluctance*, rather than his inability, to speak. We should note that Billy's possible involvement in a mutiny plot could explain two earlier questions that seem to mystify the narrator: why Billy fails to go up to the after-guardsman and "bluntly" demand "to know his purpose in the initial interview"; and why Billy does not "set about sounding some of the other impressed men of the ship in order to discover what basis, if any, there was for the emissary's obscure suggestions as to plotting disaffection aboard" (89–90). It could well be that the narrator is mystified by such questions because they seem to relate some truth that directly conflicts with his own biases, with his own idealized conception of Billy Budd.

In the same way that Melville's text questions the moral truth of the char-acters—that is, Billy and Claggart—who are seemingly allegorized in terms of good and evil, it also questions the moral truth of those who stand in judgment of morality, of those who decide the innocence and guilt of others. This is precisely what occurs in the portrayal of Captain Vere, who is faced with the difficult decision of whether to sentence the "angel of God" (101)—as he calls Billy Budd—to death for killing the "evil" Claggart. How does Vere finally arrive at his decision? What "truth" is there in the judgment he makes? It is apparent that after Billy strikes out and kills the master-at-arms in Vere's cabin, the narrator begins to organize the tragic circumstances of the story as much around Vere's decision as he does around Billy's fate (a fact that has led some critics to see Vere as the story's central character).[29] Thus the narrator summarizes the problematic posi-tion in which Vere finds himself with regard to Billy's deadly deed:

> In a legal view the apparent victim of the tragedy was he who had sought to vic-timize a man blameless; and the indisputable deed of the latter, navally regarded, constituted the most heinous of military crimes. Yet more. The essential right and wrong involved in the matter, the clearer that might be, so much the worse for the responsibility of a loyal sea commander, inasmuch as he was not authorized to determine the matter on that primitive basis. (103)

Because Vere is one who holds firmly to the belief that, where mankind is concerned, "forms, measured forms, are everything" (128), he feels he can judge Billy only in strict accordance with those forms as they are man-

---

29. Many critics view Melville's moral position in *Billy Budd* as dependent on the narrator's ironic or nonironic attitude toward Captain Vere. For a good example of this privileging of Vere's status in the text, see Dryden, *Melville's Thematics of Form*, pp. 209–16.

ifested in the present military law—a law that he, as a loyal sea commander, is sworn to uphold. But if we carefully examine the way in which Billy's
judgment is ultimately carried out, we soon discover that the "forms" by
which Vere proceeds to come to terms with Billy's violent action are themselves violations of the so-called proper forms of justice. What is supposed
to be a legal system based on fairness and reason in fact turns out to be (as
it is represented through Vere) just as violent and irrational as those forces
that the legal system is supposed to keep under control.

The narrator tells us that Vere, in trying to obey the forms or usages of
martial law, decides it would be most proper "to turn the matter [of Billy's
crime] over to a summary court of his own officers, reserving for himself,
as the one on whom the ultimate accountability would rest, the right of
maintaining a supervision of it, or formally *or informally* interposing at
need" (104, emphasis mine). Declaring that Vere is extremely attentive to
those "measured forms" around which he believes the world should be
organized, the narrator at the same time suggests that there may reside
within Vere's forms a certain degree of informality, that is, a certain undermining of forms. This subtle clue as to the true nature of Vere's formalized
conception of the world is given further emphasis when we learn that in
coordinating a group of men to constitute the drumhead court, Vere
chooses a man—an officer of the marines—who may have no right to be
part of such a formal military gathering. As the narrator points out, "In
associating an officer of marines with the sea lieutenant and the sailing
master [the other members of the court], the commander perhaps deviated
from general custom" (104).

Earlier we are made to understand, by way of the ship's surgeon's opinion, that the whole idea of setting up a summary court in the first place may
be a departure from standard procedure, an opinion completely contrary
to Vere's conviction that such an undertaking "would not be at variance
with usage" (104). Thus we hear: "As to the drumhead court, it struck the
surgeon as impolitic, if nothing more. The thing to do, he thought, was to
place Billy Budd in confinement, and in a way dictated by usage, and
postpone further action in so extraordinary a case to such a time as they
should rejoin the squadron, and then refer it to the admiral" (101). That this
opinion is not only the surgeon's but also the one shared by the lieutenants
and by the captain of marines, perhaps further supports the idea that
Vere's adherence to "forms" is not as strict as the narrator (or even as Vere
himself) would like to believe. We may add that even Billy's early-morning
execution at the yardarm, following the evening sentencing, seems to be a
deviation from the regular custom, since, as the narrator points out, "as is
customary in such cases, the sentence would forthwith have been carried
out [and not postponed until morning]" (114).

There are suggestions throughout the narrative that the drumhead court
that Vere calls on to decide Billy's fate is a weak and unreliable means of

determining justice. Not only is the captain of marines apparently ill-suited for the task of unraveling the moral dilemma that stands before him but so also are the two other members of the court, the first lieutenant and the sailing master, whose "intelligence was mostly confined to the matter of active seamanship and the fighting demands of their profession" (105). It seems that only Captain Vere commands enough legal understanding to effectively evaluate Billy's innocence or guilt; but by the same token, we should be careful to note that when Vere delivers his line of argument to the court, it is suggested that his mastery of rhetoric, his artfulness—rather than his straightforward logic—is what convinces the court to sentence Billy to death. Indeed, Vere's "*manner of saying it*, [which] showed the influence of unshared studies" (109, emphasis mine), may have easily persuaded a court such as this one, composed as it was of "men not intellectually mature" (109) and so probably uninitiated in the skillful manipulation of language.[30] Extremely convincing to the "troubled court" (113) is Vere's closing statement, which, playing on the court's deepest fears, argues that the crew of the *Bellipotent* would no doubt be provoked to mutiny if they were to witness a failure on the officers' part to carry out the full extent of the law (which would entail executing anyone who, for whatever reason, dares to perpetrate violence against a superior in rank). But, it is hinted, even if the members of the court were to see through Vere's rhetorical ploys, they would still not have disagreed with his "logical" argument, if only because they would not, for the sake of their own professional self-interest, "gainsay one . . . not less their superior in mind than in naval rank" (113). In short, the court is ready to fall silent before the voice of a higher and more powerful authority. The judgment that is finally handed down comes as a result not of the high-minded pursuit of truth and justice but of the specific political pressures that dominate the court's decision making.

But if the court that is appointed to administer justice in the Billy Budd affair proves itself to be inadequate to the task, how much more adequate is Captain Vere? No doubt we are supposed to see Vere as the embodiment of intellectuality, a man whose love for books is so great that, each time he goes to sea, he is said to bring with him a "newly replenished library, compact but of the best" (62). There would seem to be no one better suited for presiding over Billy's trial than a man of such abundant knowledge. Yet it is interesting that in addition to the narrator's apparently strong affirmation of Vere's intellectual accomplishments, we discover contrary suggestions throughout the text that Vere's "mind" is not at all an effective instrument for determining the truth, especially when it comes to matters

---

30. See Franklin, "From Empire to Empire," p. 205, who points out, "Although Vere's verbal adroitness (the opposite of Billy's tongue-tied innocence) overwhelms this trio of naval officers, to trained students of rhetoric his devious methods are blatantly specious."

of human significance. Vere may well illustrate what the narrator's old acquaintance, the "honest scholar," views as the distinction between "knowledge of the world" and "knowledge of human nature" (75). Immersed as he is in his own bookish world, and having little interest in or ability for communicating with the seamen of the *Bellipotent* on their "common" level, Vere thus appears as someone completely out of touch with the world of his fellow man—he is alienated by his intellect. That such is indeed the case is epitomized by the fact that "he seemed unmindful of the circumstance that to his bluff company such remote allusions [as those he was apt to employ in his discourse], however pertinent they might really be, were altogether alien to men whose reading was mainly confined to journals" (63).

Shown to be incapable of relating to his crew, Vere is also suggested to suffer serious difficulties with his mind, difficulties that would indicate that not all of his judgments are supported by the highest degree of rationality. We are told, for instance, that despite Vere's often practical turn of mind, he would on occasion "betray a certain dreaminess of mood."

Standing alone on the weather side of the quarter-deck, one hand holding by the rigging, he would absently gaze off at the blank sea. At the presentation to him then of some minor matter interrupting the current of his thoughts, he would show more or less irascibility; but instantly he would control it. (61)

After reading such a characterization, we may surmise that—contrary to what the narrator contends—Vere's nickname, "Starry Vere," may not be merely an affectionate term that derives from a line in one of Andrew Marvell's poems (first noticed and applied by Vere's "favorite kinsman, Lord Denton" [61]) but rather may be a term used mockingly by the other seamen to describe the absentminded or "starry" behavior that Vere sometimes demonstrated aboard ship.

Toward the end of the novel, directly following the scene in which Billy kills Claggart, we are shown that Vere may be afflicted with a condition far worse than absentmindedness. When the surgeon observes the way in which Vere reacts to Billy's deed—that is, with "unwonted agitation" and "excited exclamations"—he begins to wonder if the otherwise calm and steady captain has not actually become a bit "unhinged" (102). Because of the narrator's earlier comments about Vere's being a supremely rational individual, "thoroughly versed in the science of his profession" (60), we would find it as difficult as does the surgeon to believe that Vere could possess even the slightest "degree of aberration" (102); and yet it is precisely this possibility that is suddenly opened to debate when, in the beginning of chapter 21, the narrator remarks:

Who in the rainbow can draw the line where the violet tint ends and the orange tint begins? Distinctly we see the difference of the colors, but where exactly does the one first blendingly enter into the other? So with sanity and insanity. In pronounced cases there is no question about them. But in some supposed cases, in various degrees supposedly less pronounced, to draw the exact line of demarcation few will undertake. (102)

Whether or not Vere has really fallen into a state of insanity is, as the narrator tells us, something that "every one must determine for himself by such light as this narrative may afford" (102). Of course the narrative, as it offers only contradictory points of view, will allow no direct light to be cast on Vere's true character, so all we can do is *speculate* whether the man who ultimately decides Billy's fate is guided by the most irrational impulses.

If it is indeed possible that Vere is somehow "affected in his mind" (101), what then is to prevent us from understanding him in the same way that the narrator understands the "evil" Claggart—as a man possessed of "Natural Depravity"? We need only study the narrator's description of the depraved nature to see that no one, not even Claggart, fits this description more accurately than the "honorable" Captain Vere. The naturally depraved individual (like Vere) is "dominated by intellectuality," and seeming as he does to come from the world of civilized society, he folds himself within "the mantle of respectability" (75). But perhaps what most characterizes the depraved person, what makes him "so exceptional a nature," lies in the following description:

Though the [depraved] man's even temper and discreet bearing would seem to intimate a mind peculiarly subject to the law of reason, not the less in heart he would seem to riot in complete exemption from that law, having apparently little to do with reason further than to employ it as an ambidexter implement for effecting the irrational. That is to say: Toward the accomplishment of an aim which in wantonness of atrocity would seem to partake of the insane, he will direct a cool judgment sagacious and sound. (76)

One can easily argue that these words perfectly describe Vere, whose insane atrocity is that he puts to death an "angel of God," all the while seeming to act with "cool judgment sagacious and sound." That Vere could actually be something of a villain behind his wholly rational and virtuous exterior would seem to be further indicated by the narrator, who remarks that in Vere's attempt to keep secret from the crew the tragic circumstances of the Billy Budd affair "lurked some resemblance to the policy adopted in those tragedies of the palace which have occurred more than once in the capital founded by Peter the Barbarian" (103). And later on (during the scene of Vere's unheroic death) we find another suggestion that Vere's cool, austere appearance may have served only to conceal a more devious sort of person, one who had often "indulged in the most secret of all passions, ambition" (129). Taken together, such comments succeed in undermining whatever credibility Vere may have as a just arbiter of morality.

Since we have observed that Vere's cherished "forms" can do nothing other than reveal their own violences, and hence their own *veering* away from the truth, we may now consider if a similar observation can be made about what the narrator claims as his own form of truth, that is, the history he entitles *Billy Budd, Sailor.* In his narration "essentially having less to do with fable than with fact" (128), the narrator impresses us with the idea that he is a historian devoted to presenting, uncompromisingly, the truth of the events. Unlike other naval historians, for instance, who might "naturally abridge" (55) the more unflattering episodes of their nation's history, this narrator feels obliged to report on any and all events, however politically embarrassing they might prove to be; and it is apparently for this reason that he tells the story of the Great Mutiny at the Nore, one of the darkest chapters in the history of the British Empire. And yet, although the narrator tries to represent himself as one who will offer nothing less than a complete and comprehensive view of history (particularly of the Billy Budd affair and the important historic events that surround it), we soon come to realize that it is precisely his painstaking adherence to the facts— his will to truth—that leads, paradoxically, to his falling into error.

We may see as suggestive in this regard a statement the narrator makes in relation to his own narration, a statement that typifies his procedure in telling what he considers to be the "truth." About to digress from his main story line into a discussion of Nelson's military heroism at the battle of Trafalgar, the narrator remarks:

In this matter of writing, resolve as one may to keep to the main road, some bypaths have an enticement not readily to be withstood. I am going to err into such a bypath. If the reader will keep me company I shall be glad. At the least, we can promise ourselves that pleasure which is wickedly said to be in sinning, for a literary sin the divergence will be. (56)

Of course the specific literary sin to which the narrator alludes is not the only one to be found in *Billy Budd;* in fact, we may say that the entire narrative, from its very beginning, is characterized by the same digressive quality that we observe here in chapter 4.[31] For us, the importance of these "divergences" is that they all indicate a certain determination on the narrator's part both to come to terms with the historic events as fully as possi-

31. The first digression we observe occurs as early as the second paragraph of chapter 1, where the narrator suddenly recalls a "remarkable instance" that happened fifty years ago in Liverpool, an instance having to do with a "black pagod of a fellow" (43) who reminds us in some ways of Billy Budd.

ble (in an all-inclusive manner) *and* to follow a path to the truth that is indirect, or fictional. Indeed, it is the necessity to err, to wander from the mark, to lie, that finally becomes an integral part of the truth-telling process in *Billy Budd*. "Truth uncompromisingly told," as the narrator writes, "will always have its ragged edges" (128).

This wandering from the truth, or what we might call the fictionalization of the narrator's "history," may be said to manifest itself in the narrator's decidedly romantic or literary conception of past events. Perhaps the clearest example of this comes during the aforementioned discussion of Admiral Nelson, whose heroic action at Trafalgar the narrator begins to associate with a kind of poetic excellence. Nelson's "ornate publication" (57) of himself in battle, argues the narrator, should not be taken as something characteristic of a vain or foolhardy individual but ought rather be seen as "more heroic line in the great epics and dramas, since in such lines the poet but embodies in verse those exaltations of sentiment that a nature like Nelson, the opportunity being given, vitalizes into acts" (58). Thus as the narrator views Nelson's deed in literary terms, it is not surprising that we find him allegorizing the admiral as the Great Sailor, an appellation that, moreover, is suggested to have its derivation not in any of the narrator's historic knowledge but in an ode written by Tennyson, where the latter "invokes Nelson as 'the greatest sailor since our world began'" (58). To the narrator, Nelson represents a past that apparently had contained all the circumstances that would be conducive to romance, that is, to "knightly valor" and to "gallantry" (56), precisely the sort of circumstances that the narrator finds sadly lacking in the unpoetic present. This nostalgia for the past serves to distort the "truth" of the events on which the narrator reports and so makes of these events something akin to fiction.

As he does in the case of Admiral Nelson, the narrator also formulates his understanding of the three main characters of his history—Billy, Claggart, and Vere—according to literary models. At various moments throughout the text, Billy is compared to Adam, Hercules, Achilles, and Hyperion, names that support the narrator's idea of Billy as the embodiment of moral and physical strength. In describing Billy's one significant weakness—his stutter—the narrator compares the Handsome Sailor to "the beautiful woman in one of Hawthorne's minor tales" (53, presumably he means Georgiana in "The Birthmark"). As we have mentioned before, the narrator's reference to Billy as the Handsome Sailor calls attention to his determination to comprehend Billy on the most allegorical level, to see him less as a real historic person than as a type or as a mythical figure belonging to "the less prosaic time alike of the military and merchant navies" (43). As he states, "The form of Billy Budd was heroic" (77).[32] Clag-

---

32. Billy's representation as a heroic figure contrasts sharply with the narrator's earlier

gart, who is supposed to represent evil, seems to derive most prominently from Milton's *Paradise Lost*, as he possesses all of Satan's traits—"Pale ire, envy and despair"—when the latter approaches the Garden of Eden.[33] Not content with a solely Miltonic conception of Claggart, the narrator turns to Gothic fiction when trying to explain the cause of the master-at-arms' essential ill will, arguing that it is "as much charged with that prime element of Radcliffian romance, the mysterious, as any that the ingenuity of the author of *The Mysteries of Udolpho* could devise" (74). Hawthorne's romance *The Scarlet Letter* also seems to play a part in the narrator's characterization of Claggart. When Claggart is described as having "a red light . . . flash forth from his eye like a spark from an anvil" (88), we are suddenly reminded of the devilish Chillingworth, out of whose eyes are said to come "a glare of red light."[34] As far as Captain Vere is concerned, the narrator attempts to mediate his moral understanding of Vere through references to the Bible, specifically to Abraham and to God (both father figures). It is thus to the Judeo-Christian mythology that the narrator appeals when trying to place Vere in a more sympathetic position with regard to the "insane atrocity" committed against Billy Budd. That the narrator, in addition, contends that Vere's popular name, Starry Vere, originally came from a poem by Marvell, is perhaps another indication of the narrator's dependency on literature for the making of his "history."

With all these literary references in *Billy Budd*, it is not surprising that we find the narrator shaping his text in the same way as would a literary artist. Somewhat like Ishmael in *Moby-Dick*, the narrator here acts as a kind of stage manager, setting up his chapters as though they were scenes in a drama; indeed at one moment, as he is about to discuss the certain "passion" that operates between Billy and Claggart, he explicitly refers to the scrubbed gundeck as a "stage" (79) on which the two characters play out their respective roles. Earlier on, the *art* of the narrative is more indirectly referred to in a pun, when the occasion of Billy's first coming on board the *Bellipotent* is described as "an adventurous turn in his affairs, which promised an opening into novel scenes" (49). The man-of-war world that Billy suddenly enters and the whole world of events that the reader is about to enter can both be seen here in terms not only novel but also relating to *the* novel (more generally, fiction). This suggestion of the dissolution of the boundaries that are supposed to exist between history and fiction perhaps

remark that Billy "is not presented as a conventional hero" and that "the story in which he is the main figure is no romance" (53). Whether the narrator is deceptive or blind to his own text is a problem that never resolves itself.

33. See Matthiessen, *American Renaissance*, p. 505, who, besides making this observation, suggests that Edmund Spenser's Envy also figures importantly in Melville's conception of Claggart.

34. Nathaniel Hawthorne, *The Scarlet Letter,* in *The Centenary Edition*, 1:169.

becomes most apparent in the poetry that the narrator employs at various moments throughout his text, quoting as he does lines from Martial, Lord Tennyson, Andrew Marvell, Charles Dibdin, and the unnamed foretop-man who writes the ballad of "Billy in the Darbies," which closes the text. This poetry (a fictive discourse) may be said to be no less significant than are the narrator's "facts" for one's understanding of Billy Budd and of all the circumstances and events that surround him.

In a way, all this fictionalizing of history that we have so far observed in *Billy Budd* leads us back to the question with which we first began: how is it possible to distinguish the narrator's "inside story" from what could be called the "outside story" (or the sequel)? For when we consider what constitutes each part of the seemingly divided narrative, we begin to wonder if the one part is not really the mirror image of—or rather no different from—the other, with the supposedly outside view of the events consisting of the same sort of "fictions" (history/poetry) as the supposedly inside view of the events. But perhaps there is a more important point to recognize in this regard, namely that the "inside" story is always already *outside*, since the narrator's own point of view is constantly being mediated by other points of view, whether those views derive from old sea gossips like the Dansker, from Captain Graveling, from Squeak, from "a Baltimore Negro," from Claggart, or from Captain Vere.[35] The narrator's portrait of Billy Budd, we can say, *is* no more than all these diverse points of view. Thus what we determined to be the false representations that come in the way of the sequel—that is, the naval report and the poem—are simply the continuation of the myriad and often contradictory portrayals of Billy that have already occurred throughout the entire narrative, from the very first chapter.[36]

As there seems to be no *proper* perspective from which to view Billy Budd (and his story), we are forced to conclude that Billy's "essence" is made up entirely of the various interpretations of him given during the course of the narrative. Melville's text has succeeded not in allowing us an "inside" understanding of Billy but in making us aware of the sort of violences that accompany any interpretation, be it legal, moral, historic, scientific, or literary (however one wishes to define it). As in Nietzsche, all such *forms* of truth are in the end nothing other than the mechanism by

35. See Evans, " 'Too Good to be True,' " p. 346, who argues that "it is Vere who first characterizes Billy as innocent and Claggart as a villain," resulting in the dualistic moral scheme that "serves as the framework of his [the narrator's] narrative."

36. Contradictory portrayals of Billy occur in chapter 26, where the purser and the surgeon offer their separate views of Billy's death. The former sees Billy's "absence of spasmodic movement" (125) as a sign of the supernatural; the latter sees it as wholly explainable by the laws of science. These two views of Billy—the romantic and the realistic—may be said to represent the narrator's "own" contradictory interpretation of Billy Budd.

which certain individuals or groups seize and maintain their power in society.[37] Like the institutionalized violence that Captain Vere represents, the narrator's allegorical system of comprehending the world is marked by a lust for power, evidenced perhaps in his frequent use of the word *striking* when calling up the images of specific characters. Implicit in the narrator's statement about John Claggart—"His portrait I essay, but shall never *hit* it" (64, emphasis mine)—is precisely the kind of violence of which his activity of representing/interpreting is most capable. No less than Vere (and the British crown that Vere loyally serves), the narrator attempts through his violences and violations of the "truth" to establish a degree of authority that will not be contradicted.

In a sense we can say that in *Billy Budd* Melville seems not to have moved beyond *Moby-Dick* in terms of his skepticism about the reliability of any form of the "truth," including the form into which he put most of his artistic energy—that of fiction. With his last notable work of fiction, Melville did not, as some critics would contend, come closer to reconciling himself with the world of forms[38] but instead demonstrated himself to be even more adept, and more subtle, in his dark exploration of the ways in which forms (or languages) continually fail to approach some permanent truth. The radical skepticism—and indeterminacy—that characterize *Billy Budd* should perhaps be finally understood by the way in which the text anticipates the violent activity and the desire for power on the part of all those interpreters (meaning ourselves) who would impose their own forms, their own fictions, on the ones that have already been articulated "inside" the narrative. Indeed, far from serving to unify or complete the text of *Billy Budd*, such interpretations would only fragment it further, adding to the story more "sequels" as falsely representative as those that appear at the text's end. "[H]ence the conclusion of such a narration is apt to be less finished than an architectural finial" (128).

---

37. For a provocative discussion of the ways in which violence incorporates itself into any system of knowledge, see Michel Foucault, "Nietzsche, Genealogy, History," *Language, Counter-Memory, Practice*, trans. Donald F. Bouchard and Sherry Simon, p. 151, who argues: "Humanity does not gradually progress from combat to combat until it arrives at universal reciprocity, where the rule of law finally replaces warfare; humanity installs each of its violences in a system of rules and thus proceeds from domination to domination. . . . Rules are empty in themselves, violent and unfinalized; they are impersonal and can be bent to any purpose. The successes of history belong to those who are capable of seizing these rules." See also Barbara Johnson, "Melville's Fist: The Execution of *Billy Budd*," in *Herman Melville's Billy Budd, Benito Cereno, Bartleby the Scrivener, and Other Tales*, ed. Harold Bloom, p. 79–80: "The legal order, which attempts to submit 'brute force' to 'forms, measured forms,' can only eliminate violence by transforming violence into the final authority."

38. See Baym, "Melville's Quarrel with Fiction," p. 921: "What the final import of *Billy Budd* might have been we cannot know, but we may take it, even in its unfinished state, as the sign of a truce in Melville's quarrel with fiction."

Epilogue: HENRY JAMES AND THE CRITICAL ABYSS: *The Aspern Papers*

Throughout this study I have suggested that the literary critic becomes just as implicated in the "errors of interpretation" as do the various narrators/readers that we customarily find in the fictions of Poe, Hawthorne, and Melville. It may therefore be interesting to demonstrate, by way of conclusion, how the critic's desire for mastery over the literary text undoes itself in no less a "master" than Henry James, whose uncanny fictions may be said to extend the tradition of the earlier American writers into the twentieth century.

In James's critical prefaces to the New York edition of his fiction (1906–1908), we discover an author whose need to dominate his work becomes apparent in the many evaluative comments he makes concerning his fiction's organic structure and formal unity (exactly those Emersonian qualities that eventually find their way into New Critical discourse).[1] Indeed, James's "house of fiction," as he calls it in the preface to *The Portrait of a Lady*, though it may possess a multitude of "possible windows" looking out onto "the spreading field, the human scene," is nevertheless suggested to be an architectural totality, a unified " 'literary form' " behind which stands the "consciousness of the artist" (*AN*, 46). Like those characters in James who act as central intelligences, "intense *perceivers*" (*AN*, 71) through whose consciousness the action of the narrative is supposed to be filtered, the author or "artist" becomes a kind of interpreter of his own fiction, a self-present consciousness that engages in both discovering and maintaining the essential unity of the text. Though it is true that James recognizes the importance of creating such "intelligences" in order to give a sense of centrality to his fiction—we think of Isabel Archer, Hyacinth Robinson, Fleda Vetch, and Lambert Strether, to name only a few—there is little question as to whose consciousness, whose intelligence, is given the most privileged position. As we see in the preface to *The American*, James may well assign to his main character, Christopher Newman, the task of overseeing or interpreting the many scenes and actions of the narrative, but it is finally James himself who becomes the real critical consciousness, the real "center" of the novel:

If Newman was attaching enough, I must have argued, his tangle would be sensi-

---

1. Typical of the sort of organicism running throughout Henry James's writing is the following passage, from the preface to *What Maisie Knew*, in *The Art of the Novel* (hereafter cited in the text as *AN*), ed. R. P. Blackmur, p. 158: "The scenic passages are *wholly* and logically scenic, having for their rule of beauty the principle of the 'conduct,' the organic development, of a scene—the entire succession of values that flower and bear fruit on ground solidly laid for them."

ble enough; for the interest of everything is all that it is *his* vision, *his* conception, *his* interpretation: at the window of his wide, quite sufficiently wide, consciousness we are seated, from that admirable position we "assist." . . . A beautiful infatuation this, always, I think, the intensity of the creative effort to get into the skin of the creature; the act of personal possession of one being by another at its completest—and with the high enchancement, ever, that it is, by the same stroke, the effort of the artist to preserve for his subject that unity, and for his use of it (in other words for the interest he desires to excite) that effect of a *centre*, which most economise its value. (*AN*, 37–38)

The sort of centrality that James as a creative artist proposes for himself—as he not only stands behind and lends "assistance" to the central character but also comes to possess him completely—seems clear enough. Yet at this point, let us understand that for all of the claims that James makes in his prefaces for a center of consciousness that would control his fiction, that would serve as an interpretive and metaphysical base for it, James still, perhaps unwittingly, succeeds only in undermining the very notion of this "center," and of himself as a self-possessed, all-commanding critic of his own text. We may take as an illustrative example of James's ironization of the central interpretive consciousness (of the whole idea of "mastery") a short novel that deals explicitly with the problem of the literary critic—*The Aspern Papers*, first published in 1888 and later revised for the New York edition in 1908.

The "center of consciousness" that James employs in this narrative is a nameless critic who tries through devious means to obtain the private letters of a long-deceased American expatriate, the poet Jeffrey Aspern, the objective here being one that is typical of certain forms of literary scholarship: to "lay bare the truth" while still trying to preserve the sanctity of the god-like artist.[2] But just how possible is it for this critic-narrator to discover the truth of Jeffrey Aspern? And what exactly is the cost of such an interpretive venture? The loss of the letters at the end of the narrative—when Miss Tina, rejected in love, decides to destroy them—surely bespeaks the ultimate failure on the critic's part to "read" his beloved poet; yet we should be aware that even before this crucial moment, James's text is bent on dramatizing how the act of reading (criticism) becomes problematic from its outset, doomed as it is to subvert its own intentions toward making a full disclosure of the truth. Indeed, all of the vehicles and passageways that the critic hopes to use to acquire the prized Aspern papers (and thus "read" the poet) become as well the very obstacles that make impossible the success of his interpretive quest.

We notice, for instance, how in the great labyrinthine house of the Miss-

2. Henry James, *The Aspern Papers*, p. 90. All future references to *The Aspern Papers* pertain to this edition.

es Bordereau, "the fine architectural doors" and "the various rooms [that] repeated themselves . . . at intervals" (16) provide a path to the coveted documents yet simultaneously lead into "impenetrable regions" (16)—rooms from which the critic is barred and walls beyond which he cannot see. The middle-aged Miss Tina and her extremely old and infirmed aunt, Juliana—who is the subject of much of Aspern's love poetry—represent to the narrator the "esoteric knowledge" about Aspern for which his "critical heart" longs (44). But though he sees the Misses Bordereau as the best means of securing the "sacred relics" (43), Miss Tina turns out to be a perfectly innocent and "witless" (62) woman who, because of her blind loyalty to her aunt, does little to advance the critic's plan to obtain the papers; and Juliana, "full of craft" (86), works actively to subvert his scholarly goals, forcing the critic to pay dearly for the "campaign" (5) he conducts. Worth noting is the irony of the critic's attempt to make use of women (his confidant Mrs. Prest included) in the first place, since he suggests early in the narrative that Aspern, as he was "not a woman's poet" (5), can be properly appreciated only by such male worshipers as himself.[3]

The critic originally hopes to "get a footing" (11)—to establish himself firmly within reach of Aspern's "literary remains" (12)—by becoming a lodger in Juliana and her niece's old and dilapidated Venetian palace, whose attached garden, as he tells Miss Tina, is indispensable to his comfort and his literary pursuits. It soon becomes obvious that the garden that the critic feels compelled to "work" (15) and that he "*must* have" (17) functions as what Susanne Kappeler sees as a "metonymic displacement" of the obsessively sought-after papers.[4] Instead of drawing him closer to the object of his desire, that is, to the "treasure" (43) that would reveal the true Jeffrey Aspern, the critic's "working the garden" only moves him further away; it constantly operates as a displacing of the "truth." Indeed, since the garden is positioned next to, or *before*, the part of the house that contains the well-hidden Aspern papers, it thus becomes both literally and figuratively what the critic calls a "pretext" (11).

Here in the garden the critic "cultivates" his "plot" and in so doing turns what we might ordinarily think of as a natural place into the site of art and deception, a place where the critic can practice his fiction. Besides being the locale where he initiates his devilish attempts to seduce the innocent Miss Tina into obtaining for him the precious documents, the garden also becomes a sort of library, furnished with the critic's low table and armchair, with his "books and portfolios," with all that would be required to carry

3. The narrator's phallocentric ideology becomes clear in the novel's first paragraph, where he says: "It is not supposed easy for women to rise to the large free view of anything, anything to be done" (3). See John Carlos Rowe's feminist reading of the novel in *The Theoretical Dimensions of Henry James*, pp. 104–18.
4. Susanne Kappeler, *Writing and Reading in Henry James*, p. 34.

on his usual "business of writing" (45). And though he does spend much of his time here musing on his covert "campaign," he likewise finds amid his newly blossomed flowers an atmosphere ripe for hatching romances and "spinning theories" (48), if not about Jeffrey Aspern then about the poet's primary source of inspiration, his mistress Juliana. Thus the arbour in which the critic has succeeded in installing himself becomes the place where Aspern's life (as well as that life—Juliana's—inextricably bound to it) is not so much comprehended as it is invented, "spun" out or fictionalized, to complete that idealized portrait of the poet that the critic most desires to see. Like the "horrible green shade" (23) that Juliana wears over her failing eyes and like the green box (105) in which Aspern's papers are concealed—both, in their greenness, symbolizing what is "natural" and hence what is "true"—the garden of the Misses Bordereau serves less as a vehicle for knowing the truth about Aspern than as a barrier or, more precisely, as a border that would permanently separate the critic from any "inside" knowledge—or from any knowledge that is inside the house (in this sense the name of the two spinsters, Bordereau, is suggestive of the critic's problem).

Because the critic's desire to "read" Jeffrey Aspern can result only in his own invention of the poet's life—a fictionalization—we can thus say that the Aspern papers that he tries to obtain are precisely those papers he has come to compose, The Aspern Papers, the narrative that we are now reading. This suggests that the narrator-critic has been, all along, placing himself in the position of Aspern, in effect attempting to identify with him to the extent of usurping the poet's life or, let us say, of trying to repeat it. Our first indication that such is the case is when the critic, conjecturing on how Aspern may have treated some of his more unreasonable women admirers, tries to imagine himself "in his [Aspern's] place—if I could imagine myself in any such a box" (7), thus calling attention to the box of letters that contains the poet's "essence." Later on, the critic admits to feeling the spirit of Aspern, which keeps "perpetual company" with him and assumes the role of his "prompter":

I had invoked him and he had come; he hovered before me half the time; it was as if his bright ghost had returned to earth to assure me he regarded the affair [of obtaining the letters] as his own no less than as mine and that we should see it fraternally and fondly to a conclusion. (42)

Sensing a "mystic companionship, a moral fraternity with all those who in the past had been in the service of art," the critic clearly sees himself as a kind of artist figure whose muse is Jeffrey Aspern; and so now, longing to have his life be continuous with Aspern's, he is determined to share in "the general romance and the general glory" (43) that was once the domain of that most illustrious expatriated American poet. In a virtual playing out of the scenario of Aspern's life, the critic becomes an American man of letters who has gone abroad and who is now making love to—or, more accurately, seducing—Juliana's more innocent counterpart, Miss Tina (who could well be not Juliana's niece but rather her illegitimate daughter by Aspern). That the critic, throughout the course of his Venetian sojourn, consistently deceives and finally spurns Miss Tina does not necessarily undermine the parallel with Aspern's love affair with Juliana, as we learn early that according to certain "impressions" (none of which the critic can allow himself to believe, so inclined is he to idealize Aspern), the esteemed poet had "treated her [Juliana] badly, just as . . . he had 'served' . . . several other ladies in the same masterful way" (7).

The attempt on the critic-narrator's part to "get into the skin" of his beloved poet may well suggest to us the sort of subjective reading by a central consciousness that James characteristically insists on. But, we may ask, what possibility exists for the critic to be metaphysically *present*—that is, a subject—when his life is so bound up in his other, Jeffrey Aspern (someone whom he has for the most part invented in the first place)? In this world of literature to which he devotes himself, it becomes apparent that while displacing the object of his study he cannot help but displace himself as well, distancing himself as he does from what he would like to know as his own subjective center, his "critical heart."

His loss of a stable position for himself may be said to be emblematized toward the end of the narrative, when, floating aimlessly along the Venetian canals in his gondola, he begins to view the city as "an immense collective apartment," a "splendid common domicile, familiar domestic and resonant." In the Piazza San Marco he envisions an "ornamental corner" and in the palaces and churches "divans of repose" (140). Though such images appear to convey a sense of security, one must realize that the critic here is, more importantly, losing his "ground," experiencing as he does the uncanny collapse of those territorial boundaries that might otherwise be recognizable, that is, the inside and the outside (apartment interiors and city "streets").[5] Moreover, what makes his "position" doubly bizarre is the fact that the seemingly "familiar" and "domestic" landscape in which he finds himself *simultaneously* takes on the unreal, the fictive, aspect of a "theatre with its actors clicking over the bridges," the footways that edge the canals assuming "the importance of a stage." Indeed, by the end of his visionary voyage through the "streets" of Venice, the critic's "home" of a city is shown to strangely transform itself into "little houses of comedy" (140). Such a lack of a sense of place, of a sense of centeredness,

5. For a discussion of "territories" in the novel, see Rosemary F. Franklin, "The Military Metaphors and the Organic Structure of Henry James's 'The Aspern Papers.' " I would argue, against Franklin, that the military metaphors call attention not to formal unity but to violence, rupture, and difference in James's text.

may remind us that the old palace in which the critic tries to center himself—and which also becomes his center of interest—is said to be, in
Juliana's very first, consequential words, "very far from the centre" (25).
Neither can the critic "get a footing" with respect to Aspern or with
respect to his own "self."

As the critic in James's story fails to establish himself as a subject, as a
center of consciousness, we may now wonder how James himself can
maintain a "central" position, can hold his ground as a critical consciousness that would have mastery over, as well as bring unity to, the
text. It is in the critical preface to *The Aspern Papers* that James tries to represent himself as an authorial presence or an originating consciousness.
Here, as in many of his prefaces, he attempts to locate the "germ" of his
narrative, that special moment or set of circumstances in the past that gave
rise to the story. Thus he begins his preface: "I not only recover with ease,
but I delight to recall, the first impulse given to the idea of 'The Aspern
Papers'" (*AN*, 159).

The origin of the story, James argues, is related not to any situation that
he might have "'found'" but to one that he was able to recognize once it
presented itself to him, as if "'literary history' . . . had in an out-of-the-
way corner of the great garden of life thrown off a curious flower that I was
to feel worth gathering as soon as I saw it. I got wind of my positive fact, I
followed the scent" (*AN*, 159). In a certain way we are reminded here of
how Hawthorne claims to have come upon his story of *The Scarlet Letter* in
a rag of scarlet cloth that, in availing itself to his sympathetic understanding, communicated "some deep meaning." For James, the "positive fact"
whose scent he follows is not an object of cloth but a woman named Jane
Clairmont, who was once Byron's mistress. Clairmont, in the "mere strong
fact" of her still living and thus of her testifying for "the reality and the
closeness of our relation to the past" (*AN*, 162), provides James with the
essential ingredient for his story concerning the reclusive mistress of that
"American Byron" (*AN*, 166) Jeffrey Aspern.[6]

But if the presence of Jane Clairmont in Florence (where James is resid-
ing at the time) is supposed to provide the perceived origin of his story, we
might do well to notice how James succeeds only in ironizing this "origin"
by making it completely imperceptible, by placing it at such a distance that
for it ever to be "perceived" it must first be *invented*. For James it becomes
important to keep this vestige of the "Byronic age" (*AN*, 165)—Miss Clairmont—"preciously unseen" in order not to run the risk of "depreciating

6. Though James cites Miss Clairmont's presence in Italy as the most essential "fact," he
also points out that two additional items were important to his story, one having to do with
an "ardent Shelleyite" who failed to obtain certain Shelley documents from Miss Clairmont
and the other concerning "a younger female relative of the ancient woman" (*AN*, 162–63).

that romance-value" that her long survival assures. Indeed, her potential for being rendered into artistic form becomes all the greater if she is left unapproached and unread, for as James believes, he would have little to gain by "pretending to read meanings into things [i.e., Miss Clairmont] absolutely sealed and beyond test or proof—to tap a fount of waters that couldn't possibly not have run dry" (*AN*, 161–62). Interested less in accumulating facts than in what he shall "add to them" and how he shall "turn them" (*AN*, 163), James thus keeps himself at a far remove from his story's most original "fact."

When at one moment in the text James speaks of the "palpable imaginable *visitable* past," he seems to be referring to the way in which Miss Clairmont's presence signals a continuity with a previous historic period; but his language, as we notice, is general enough that it may relate as well to his own desire to establish, here in the preface, a continuity with the *story's* past, with *its* origins. Here he draws the analogy between trying to appreciate, or know, the past at too many removes and looking over a garden wall:

With more moves back the element of the appreciable shrinks—just as the charm of looking over a garden-wall into another garden breaks down when successions of walls appear. The other gardens, those still beyond, may be there, but even by use of our longest ladder we are baffled and bewildered—the view is mainly a view of barriers. (*AN*, 164)

What James is describing here is the difficulty of ever recovering the origin of his narrative, of ever laying bare the secret truth of his story; for as it is suggested early in the preface, there is nothing but barriers, one after another, to subvert whatever "revisiting, re-appropriating impulse" James may have. Seeking that "general impression" of Florence that was supposed to help give rise to his story, James compares the entertaining of this impression to "the fashion of our intercourse with Iberians or Orientals" whose form of courtesy is such that "we peep at most into two or three of the chambers of their hospitality, with the rest of the case stretching beyond our ken and escaping our penetration" (*AN*, 160). The sense that multiple barriers stand in the way of making palpable or visitable that past wherein the story was born is further emphasized when James, envisioning past settings, sees "in too thick and rich a retrospect . . . my old Venice of 'The Aspern Papers,' . . . the still earlier one of Jeffrey Aspern himself, and . . . even the comparatively recent Florence that was to drop into my ear the solicitation of these things" (*AN*, 161). Each of these remembrances simply serves as another "wall" that obscures James's view of that "garden" in which his story truly began.[7]

7. We may well view Jeffrey Aspern here as a barrier to truth if we consider that "behind him" stands the poet Byron and behind Byron probably a long line of romantics that includes even such fictitious lovers as Shakespeare's Italian, Romeo (52)

The final barrier that James must confront is, ironically enough, the very preface that he is writing; for instead of acting as a kind of critical-historic foundation for his narrative, it becomes but another fiction, in some ways no different from the story it is supposed to introduce. James seems in his preface almost to repeat the quest of his narrator-critic in the story, searching as he does for the truth of his "papers," trying to link them with some previous moment in history. The images of garden walls and impenetrable chambers, all of which play such an important role in the narrator's plight, reappear in the preface, serving James in the same way as they do the narrator-critic: as representations of the obstacles that would prevent one from ever determining the truth of the text. Because James imports the basic elements of his fictional discourse into his own critical preface, it is no longer possible to discern where the boundaries between fiction and criticism properly lie. Decentering himself as a "center of consciousness," as a self-same critical mind that stands *before* the book (originating and dominating it), James thus reduces to a fairy tale the notion that—as he says in another preface—"to criticise is to appreciate, to appropriate, to take intellectual possession, to establish in fine a relation with the criticised thing and make it one's own" (*AN*, 155).

BIBLIOGRAPHY

Allison, David B., ed. *The New Nietzsche: Contemporary Styles of Interpretation.* New York: Dell Publishing Co., 1979.

Babbit, Irving. *Rousseau and Romanticism.* Boston: Houghton Mifflin Co., 1919.

Bales, Kent. "Sexual Exploitation and the Fall from Natural Virtue in Rappaccini's Garden." *ESQ* 24 (1978): 133–44.

Barthes, Roland. *Image-Music-Text.* Trans. Stephen Heath. New York: Hill and Wang, 1977.

Basler, Roy P. "Byronism in Poe's 'To One in Paradise.'" *American Literature* 9 (1937): 232–36.

Baym, Nina. "Melville's Quarrel with Fiction." *PMLA* 94, no. 5 (October 1979): 909–23.

———. "The Romantic *Malgré Lui:* Hawthorne in 'The Custom House.'" *ESQ* 19 (1973): 14–25.

Beaver, Harold. Introduction to *Billy Budd, Sailor and Other Stories.* Middlesex: Penguin Books, 1983.

Benton, Richard P. "Is Poe's 'The Assignation' a Hoax?" *Nineteenth Century Fiction* 18 (1963): 193–97.

Bersani, Leo. *Baudelaire and Freud.* Berkeley: University of California Press, 1977.

Blanchot, Maurice. *The Gaze of Orpheus.* Trans. Lydia Davis. New York: Station Hill Press, 1981.

Bloom, Harold. *A Map of Misreading.* New York: Oxford University Press, 1975.

Bonaparte, Marie. *The Life and Works of Edgar Allan Poe: A Psycho-Analytic Interpretation.* Trans. John Rodker. London: Hogarth Press, 1949.

Borges, Jorge Luis. *Labyrinths: Selected Stories and Other Writings.* Ed. Donald A. Yates and James E. Irby. New York: New Directions, 1964.

Brodtkorb, Paul, Jr. "The Definitive *Billy Budd:* 'But Aren't it all Sham?'" *PMLA* 82, no. 7 (Dec. 1967): 602–12.

Coward, Rosalind, and John Ellis. *Language and Materialism.* London: Routledge and Kegan Paul, 1977.

Crews, Frederick. *The Sins of the Fathers: Hawthorne's Psychological Themes.* New York: Oxford University Press, 1966.

———, ed. *The Great Short Works of Nathaniel Hawthorne.* New York: Harper and Row Publishers, 1967.

Culler, Jonathan. *Ferdinand de Saussure.* New York: Penguin Books, 1977.

Dauber, Kenneth. "Criticism of American Literature." *Diacritics* 7, no. 1 (Spring 1977): 55–66.

———. "The Problem of Poe." *Georgia Review* 32, no. 3 (Fall 1978): 645–57.

Davidson, Edward H. *Poe: A Critical Study.* Cambridge: Harvard University Press, 1966.

De Man, Paul. *Allegories of Reading: Figural Language in Rousseau, Nietzsche, Rilke, and Proust.* New Haven: Yale University Press, 1979.

————. *Blindness and Insight: Essays in the Rhetoric of Contemporary Criticism.* Minneapolis: University of Minnesota Press, 1983.

————. "Intentional Structure of the Romantic Image." In *Romanticism and Consciousness*, ed. Harold Bloom. New York: W. W. Norton and Company, 1970.

Derrida, Jacques. "Fors." Trans. Barbara Johnson. *Georgia Review* 31, no. 1 (Spring 1977): 64–116.

————. *Of Grammatology.* Trans. Gayatri Spivak. Baltimore: Johns Hopkins University Press, 1976.

————. *Positions.* Trans. Alan Bass. Chicago: University of Chicago Press, 1981.

————. "The Purveyor of Truth." Trans. Willis Domingo et al. *Yale French Studies* 52 (1975): 31–113.

————. "White Mythology." Trans. F.C.T. Moore. *New Literary History* 6, no. 1 (Autumn 1974): 5–74.

Donato, Eugenio. "The Ruins of Memory: Archeological Fragments and Textual Artifacts." *Modern Language Notes* 93, no. 4 (May 1978): 575–96.

Dryden, Edgar A. *Melville's Thematics of Form.* Baltimore: Johns Hopkins University Press, 1968.

————. *Nathaniel Hawthorne: The Poetics of Enchantment.* Ithaca: Cornell University Press, 1977.

Emerson, Ralph Waldo. *The Collected Works of Ralph Waldo Emerson.* 4 vols. Ed. Robert E. Spiller and Alfred R. Ferguson. Cambridge: Harvard University Press, 1971–.

————. *Journals of Ralph Waldo Emerson.* 10 vols. Ed. Edward Waldo Emerson and Waldo Emerson Forbes. Boston: Houghton Mifflin Company, 1909–1914.

Evans, Lyon, Jr. " 'Too Good to be True': Subverting Christian Hope in *Billy Budd.*" *New England Quarterly* 55, no. 3 (Sept. 1982): 323–53.

Feidelson, Charles, Jr. *Symbolism and American Literature.* Chicago: University of Chicago Press, 1953.

Fiedler, Leslie A. *Love and Death in the American Novel.* New York: Stein and Day, 1966.

Fisher IV, Benjamin Franklin. "To 'The Assignation' from 'The Visionary' and Poe's Decade of Revising." *Library Chronicle* 39 (1973): 89–105.

————. "To 'The Assignation' from 'The Visionary' (Part Two): The Revisions and Related Matters." *Library Chronicle* 40 (1976): 221–51.

Foucault, Michel. *Language, Counter-Memory, Practice.* Trans. Donald F. Bouchard and Sherry Simon. Ithaca: Cornell University Press, 1977.

————. *The Order of Things: An Archaeology of the Human Sciences.* New York: Random House, 1970.

Foust, R. E. "Aesthetician of Simultaneity: E. A. Poe and Modern Literary Theory." *South Atlantic Review* 46, no. 2 (May 1981): 17–25.

Frank, Frederick S. "Poe's House of the Seven Gothics: The Fall of the Narrator in 'The Fall of the House of Usher.' " *Orbis Litterarum* 34, no. 4 (1979): 331–51.

Franklin, H. Bruce. *The Wake of the Gods: Melville's Mythology.* Stanford: Stanford University Press, 1963.

Franklin, Rosemary F. "The Military Metaphors and the Organic Structure of Henry James's 'The Aspern Papers.' " *Arizona Quarterly* 32, no. 4 (Winter 1976): 327–40.

Franzosa, John. "The Language of Inflation in 'Rappaccini's Daughter.' " *Texas Studies in Literature and Language* 24, no. 1 (Spring 1982): 1–22.

Freud, Sigmund. "The Uncanny." In Vol 17 of *The Standard Edition of the Complete Psychological Works of Sigmund Freud*, ed. James Strachey. London: Hogarth Press, 1955.

Frye, Northrop, ed. *Romanticism Reconsidered*. New York: Columbia University Press, 1963.

Girgus, Sam. "Poe and R.D. Laing: The Transcendental Self." *Studies in Short Fiction* 13, no. 3 (Summer 1976): 299–309.

Guetti, Barbara Jones. "Resisting the Aesthetic." *Diacritics* 17, no. 1 (Spring 1987): 33–45.

Harari, Josue V., ed. *Textual Strategies: Perspectives in Post-Structuralist Criticism*. Ithaca: Cornell University Press, 1979.

Hawthorne, Nathaniel. *The House of the Seven Gables*. Vol. 3 of *The Complete Works of Nathaniel Hawthorne*. Boston: Houghton Mifflin Company, 1909.

———. *The Marble Faun*. Vol 4 of *The Centenary Edition of the Works of Nathaniel Hawthorne*, ed. William Charvat, Roy Harvey Pearce, and Claude Simpson. Columbus: Ohio State University Press, 1962–.

———. "Rappaccinni's Daughter." Vol. 10 of *The Centenary Edition*.

———. *The Scarlet Letter*. Vol. 1 of *The Centenary Edition*.

———. "Young Goodman Brown." Vol. 10 of *The Centenary Edition*.

Herrmann, Claudine, and Nicholas Kostis. " 'The Fall of the House of Usher' or The Art of Duplication." *Sub-Stance* 26 (1980): 36–42.

Hoffman, Daniel. *Poe Poe Poe Poe Poe Poe Poe*. New York: Doubleday and Co., 1972.

Hoffman, Michael J. "The House of Usher and Negative Romanticism." *Studies in Romanticism* 4 (1965): 158–68.

Hoffmann, E.T.A. *Weird Tales*. Trans. J. T. Bealby. New York: Scribner and Co., 1923.

Holland, Laurence Bedwell. *The Expense of Vision: Essays on the Craft of Henry James*. Princeton: Princeton University Press, 1964.

Irwin, John T. *American Hieroglyphics: The Symbol of the Egyptian Hieroglyphics in the American Renaissance*. New Haven: Yale University Press, 1980.

James, Henry. *The Aspern Papers*. New York Edition of *The Novels and Tales of Henry James*. New York: Charles Scribner's Sons, 1908.

———. Critical prefaces to *The Novels and Tales of Henry James*. In *The Art of the Novel*, ed. R. P. Blackmur. Boston: Northeastern University Press, 1984.

Johnson, Barbara. "Melville's Fist: The Execution of *Billy Budd*." In *Herman Melville's Billy Budd, Benito Cereno, Bartleby the Scrivener, and Other Tales*, ed. Harold Bloom. New York: Chelsea House Publishers, 1987.

Kappeler, Susanne. *Writing and Reading in Henry James*. London: MacMillan Press, 1980.

Lacan, Jacques. *Écrits: A Selection*. Trans. Alan Sheridan. New York: W. W. Norton and Company, 1977.

———. "The Mirror-phase as Formative of the Function of the I." Trans. Jean Roussel. *New Left Review* 51 (1968): 71–77.

———. "Seminar on 'The Purloined Letter.' " Trans. Jeffrey Mehlman. *Yale French Studies* 48 (1972): 39–72.

Lee, A. Robert, ed. *Herman Melville: Reassessments*. London: Vision Press, 1984.

Levine, Stuart, and Susan Levine. *Poe's Short Fiction*. Indianapolis: Bobbs-Merrill Co., 1976.

Macksey, Richard, and Eugenio Donato. *The Structuralist Controversy*. Baltimore: Johns Hopkins University Press, 1972.

Male, Roy. "Hawthorne and the Concept of Sympathy." *PMLA* 68, no. 1 (March 1953): 138–49.

———. *Hawthorne's Tragic Vision*. New York: W. W. Norton and Co., 1957.

Matheson, Terence J. "A New Look at Claggart." *Studies in Short Fiction* 17, no. 4 (Fall 1980): 445–53.

Matthiessen, F. O. *American Renaissance: Art and Expression in the Age of Emerson and Whitman*. New York: Oxford University Press, 1941.

Melville, Herman. *Billy Budd, Sailor (An Inside Narrative)*. Ed. Harrison Hayford and Merton Sealts, Jr. Chicago: Chicago University Press, 1962.

———. *Moby-Dick*. Norton Critical Edition. Ed. Harrison Hayford and Hershel Parker. New York: W. W. Norton and Company, 1967.

———. *Pierre, or The Ambiguities*. Vol. 7 of *The Writings of Herman Melville*. Ed. Leon Howard and Hershel Parker. Evanston and Chicago: Northwestern University Press and Newberry Library, 1971.

———. *Redburn*. Vol. 4 of *The Writings of Herman Melville*.

———. *White-Jacket, or The World in a Man-of-War*. Vol. 5 of *The Writings of Herman Melville*.

Miller, J. Hillis. "The Disarticulation of the Self in Nietzsche." *Monist* 64, no. 1 (Jan. 1981): 247–61.

———. "Steven's Rock and Criticism as Cure." *Georgia Review* 30 (Spring 1976): 5–31.

———. "Tradition and Difference." *Diacritics* 2, no. 4 (Winter 1972): 6–13.

Milton, John. *Paradise Lost*. In *The Complete Poems and Major Prose of Milton*, ed. Merrit Y. Hughes. Indianapolis: Odyssey Press, 1957.

Morison, Samuel Eliot, Henry Steele Commager, and William E. Leuchtenburg. *The Growth of the American Republic*. 2 vols. New York: Oxford University Press, 1969.

Nietzsche, Friedrich. *The Gay Science*. Trans. Walter Kaufmann. New York: Random House, 1974.

———. *On the Genealogy of Morals*. Trans. Walter Kaufmann. New York: Random House, 1967.

———. *Twilight of the Idols and the Anti-Christ*. Trans. R. J. Hollingdale. Middlesex: Penguin Books, 1968.

———. *The Will to Power*. Trans. Walter Kaufmann and R. J. Hollingdale. New York: Random House, 1967.

Norford, Don Parry. "Rappaccini's Garden of Allegory." *American Literature* 50, no. 2 (May 1978): 167–86.

Ovid. *The Metamorphoses*. Trans. Rolfe Humphries. Bloomington: Indiana University Press, 1955.

Pancost, David W. "Hawthorne's Epistemology and Ontology." *ESQ* 19 (1973): 8–13.

Pitcher, Edward. "Poe's 'The Assignation': A Reconsideration." *Poe Studies* 13, no. 1 (June 1980): 1–4.

Poe, Edgar Allan. "The Assignation." In Vol. 2 of *Collected Works of Edgar Allan Poe*, ed. Thomas Ollive Mabbott. Cambridge: Harvard University Press, 1978.

———. "The Fall of the House of Usher." In Vol. 2 of *Collected Works*.

———. "MS. Found in a Bottle." In Vol. 2 of *Collected Works*.

———. *The Narrative of Arthur Gordon Pym*. In Vol. 1 of *Collected Writings of Edgar Allan Poe*, ed. Burton R. Pollin. Boston: Twayne Publishers, 1981.

———. "The Philosophy of Composition." In Vol. 14 of *The Complete Works of Edgar Allan Poe*, ed. James A. Harrison. New York: AMS Press, 1965.

———. Review of Hawthorne's *Twice-told Tales*. In Vol. 13 of *The Complete Works*.

———. "The System of Doctor Tarr and Professor Fether." In Vol. 3 of *Collected Works*.

Poulet, Georges. *The Metamorphosis of the Circle*. Trans. Carley Dawson and Elliot Coleman. Baltimore: Johns Hopkins University Press, 1966.

Quinn, Arthur H. *Edgar Allan Poe: A Critical Biography*. New York: Appleton, 1941.

Rees, John O., Jr. "Hawthorne's Concept of Allegory: A Reconsideration." *Philological Quarterly* 54, no. 2 (1975): 494–510.

Regan, Robert, ed. *Poe: A Collection of Critical Essays*. Englewood Cliffs, N.J.: Prentice-Hall, 1967.

Ricardou, Jean. "The Singular Character of the Water." Trans. Frank Towne. *Poe Studies* 9, no. 1 (June 1976): 1–6.

Riddel, Joseph. "The 'Crypt' of Edgar Poe." *Boundary 2* 7 (Spring 1979): 117–44.

Roussel, Jean. "Introduction to Jacques Lacan." *New Left Review* 51 (1968): 63–70.

Rowe, John Carlos. *Henry Adams and Henry James: The Emergence of a Modern Consciousness*. Ithaca: Cornell University Press, 1976.

———. *Through the Custom House: Nineteenth-Century American Fiction and Modern Theory*. Baltimore: Johns Hopkins University Press, 1982.

———. *The Theoretical Dimensions of Henry James*. Madison: University of Wisconsin Press, 1984.

———. "Writing and Truth in Poe's *The Narrative of Arthur Gordon Pym*." *Glyph* 2 (1977): 102–21.

Saussure, Ferdinand de. *Course in General Linguistics*. Trans. Wade Baskin. New York: McGraw-Hill, 1966.

Soule, George H., Jr. "Byronism in Poe's 'Metzengerstein' and 'William Wilson.'" *ESQ* 24 (1978): 152–62.

Tatar, Maria. "The Houses of Fiction: Toward a Definition of the Uncanny." *Comparative Literature* 33, no. 2 (Spring 1981): 167–82.

Thompson, G. R. *Poe's Fiction: Romantic Irony in the Gothic Tales*. Madison: University of Wisconsin Press, 1973.

Thompson, Lawrance. *Melville's Quarrel with God*. Princeton: Princeton University Press, 1952.

Watson, E. L. Grant. "Melville's Testament of Acceptance." *New England Quarterly* 6 (June 1933): 319–27.

Wells, Daniel. "Engraved Within the Hills: Further Perspectives on the Ending of *Pym*." *Poe Studies* 10, no. 1 (June 1977): 13–15.

INDEX